# How to have willpower
## (and to defeat vices)

**Psychology of the Conduct:**
**to stop squandering, smoking, drinking, fattening, gambling...**

## Cacildo Marques

Cover design by Cacildo Marques
Episteme-Ed-Butantan

**ISBN: 978-1519193797**

# Contents

# How to have willpower
## (and to defeat vices)

Psychology of the Conduct: to stop squandering, smoking, drinking, fattening, gambling...

**Cacildo Marques**

The pillar of the willpower is the support of friends.

# Chapter 1. Wastefulness

The motivation to write this book came from the fact of there being so many simple persons, without resources, plunged into the breach of contract, after falling in the illusion of the easy credit plan. Obviously, it is necessary to have determination not only to escape the purchases that are besides the capacity, but also to be free of the vices, to obtain success in the studies, to be released of a destructive passion, to complete the begun works and to reach any viable objectives in whose direction the person has decided to walk.

But the credit plan is only one of the forms so that the person can be entangled in economical trouble. There are those who, even without buying on credit, spend everything what they have before the hour and remain the whole rest of the month with their cash reduced to zero. There are those who lend what they have to friends or known persons and they do not receive when they wait to dispose of the turn of that resource. This last case is not even a question of own willpower, but of naivety, or of "soft heart", which damages the owner of this organ.

"Pindaiba" (*Duguetia lanceolata*) means in Tupi "tree of fishing". It is a tree of fine trunk that natives cut to do stick of fishing. On that individual who was returning of the fishery with the stick in the back and without any fish it was said that he was returning "in the pindaiba". From there, to be "in the pindaiba" means, still today, to be broke, without resources. And the one who is "in the pindaiba" can be in this situation or because of having gained nothing or because of having lost everything. For avoiding this second case, we can receive three types of advice: do not be silly - of falling in the conversation of the most clever persons -, do not be unprepared - for being not stolen -, do not be wasteful - i.e., uses your willpower to get to administer your goods, without squandering.

The first demonstration that someone can give of having willpower is to be not a spendthrift. Being able to regulate, being able to economize, this is a display of maturity and responsibility.

*Interest.* Can I go into debt relying on simple interest?

A first question on the mermaid's chant of the credit plan is the mathematical aspect of the interest. Strangely, the chapter on compound interest does not take part still of the mathematical program of our basic teaching, but only that of simple interest, something that leads to a very damaging confusion. In the formula of simple interest, the interest is calculated multiplying linearly the initial capital by the interest rate and this total by the time of application. If the time quadruples, the interest quadruples, for example. Now, the only situation of market in what we use this type of calculation is in the discount of duplicates by banks, for a question of easiness and urgency. In all of the other cases, the interest is compound; whatever it will be the chart to be used.

In the compound interest, the capitalization is done to each period, and the interest happens on the up-to-date amount. Be supposed a capital of 1000 unities devoted to a tax of 1% per month. In the first month, the amount will be 1010 unities. In the second month the tax is not applied on the base 1000 unities, but on the amount 1010. After 36 months, the thing is difficult, when treating on a debt. This is the problem of the public debt of countries; because, in many cases, instead knocking down the debt, the government sweats to pay only the interest.

The usual formula of compound interest allows calculating, in the reality, the amount of the debt, in the determined time. In order that this amount is obtained, we multiply the capital by the power whose base is the sum of 100% plus the interest rate and whose exponent is the quantity of months, or years, according to the periodization is in one or in another measure. In the application above, after 36 months the amount will be calculated so: after adding 100% plus 1%, when 101% is obtained, or 1.01, once 100% is the same thing as 100/100, we approach to the total when the multiplication of 1000 is done by the power 1.01 lifted up to 36. This gives 1,430.77. In simple interest this would give only 1,036.00. See the difference.

Now suppose the purchasing of a bicycle of 1,000.00, but with interest of 3% in a debt of 36 monthly installments. The amount will be of 2,898.28, almost three times the cash price.

A great step in order that we acquire willpower is, so, the knowledge of the processes that can delude us.

Now look at the positive side of this system. Instead of borrowing and owing amounts at compound interest, instead of buying on the installment plan with installments to lose sight, but never with simple interest, look to be from another side of the balcony. That difference in the value of the bicycle, of 1,000.00 for 2,898.28, will be yours. If you lend 1,000.00 to someone with compound interest of 3% per month, you will have 1,898.28 of interest at the end of three years. Is there the risk of loss because of the breach of contract of other? It exists, yes. And it will exist so much the bigger the misinformation of this other person will be. So, unless you are ready for using the judicial resources to guarantee the receiving of what belongs to you, it is not suitable to lend or to sell on credit on basis of the ignorance of the client. Alerting about how much he will owe while months pass is a question of polite attitude. If he will want to make the deal even so, you know that what will take place in the future regarding values will not be a surprise.

When the persons are reasonably informed about the role of the interest, the banks use this fact to determine superior limits of the "spread", the taxes collected by them on the loans. If a client accepts to pay a very high tax, this can be a sign of that he will not carry out the agreement. Then the risk of the transaction has a ceiling for the interest rate, besides which the banks know that it is not worthwhile to lend. This is a conclusion of one of the studies of economist Joseph Stiglitz, who uses, normally, the market of the United States, where the adolescents have some formation in interest, because of a subject matter of the secondary education called 'annuities'. In markets of the Latin America, where the majority only studied of interest the part of simple interest, by a great irresponsibility of the school system, a client who accepts to pay enormous interest can be a person absolutely honest, but naive. It is not so strange, so, that when the basic tax of the government is in 12% per year, or around this, the interest of market in the credit card reach annual 180%, i. e., while you receive 12% of annual interest to be lent to the government, the credit card financiers collect 180% of you. Let's see: your neighbor bought 1,000.00 in titles of the National Treasure in January, and, in the same time, you were owing 1,000.00 in the card. In January of the next year, you owe 2,800.00 to the market, while your neighbor has amount of 1,120.00 in the hand of the government. Your neighbor won little, because of having lent to the government, with somewhat risk, because, he being not a banker, has not legal support to apply "spread" in his working capital and to go out lending in the market at high interest. But your debt accumulated in credit card was to the stratosphere. Is this unfair? It is, only in so far as we live in a world in which "there is no free lunch". The rules are these. It suits to the person to inform himself, to be prevented and to do good choices.

*Consumption.* On purchases, which should be my best strategy?

It is difficult to overthrow the impulse of buying so many irresistible products that the industry releases all the time. Who uses to economize and to look for the cheaper goods has not this type of preoccupation. Two facts are always taken into account: firstly, new and very wanted products are expensive because they are rare, like it is the case of the 'tablet' in the first months of its launching, having a tendency to lower the price with the increase of the items in the market, and, secondly, the brand is a psychological appeal, against which the person has always to be alert. Persons know that industries of wine and garments usually use two labels for the same product, one to sell expensively, for few ones, and other one to sell cheaply, aiming to reach a more numerous market. A Canadian psychologist published work recently showing that persons who drink wine with label of expensive wine find the product tastier than persons who drink the same wine, but that comes in bottle of cheap wine.

He who wants to be parsimonious, so, waits the price to go down, while keeps on using his old product, and, while seeing himself under the temptation of buying an expensive commodity, investigates if the same item is not being offered at the side under a cheaper label. You can check this in the racks of the supermarkets. The product "of own brand" usually is cheaper, by the conditions of buying before the supplier. Between two packets of biscuit, one of both them with the own brand of the supermarket and other with a traditional name of biscuits brand, search to check the address of the factory. There are cases in which the product of the traditional brand presents a price 50% bigger than that of own brand and while looking in the packing we note that both are manufactured in the same address. An inquiry of years ago showed that the preference for the own brand is in the B class, whereas the C and D classes prefer to buy the traditional brands. This can have several explanations, but the first one that we should consider is the level of information, which is, obviously, bigger in the B class than in the C and D classes, no matter what this scale means.

The Ministry of Education of Brazil decided in the beginning of 2011 to recommend to the systems of teaching that notions of financial mathematics were introduced in the schools of secondary education, as "cross" subject, i. e., theme being explored in several subject matters, but not like specific chapter. In spite of the preoccupation of the Ministry being praiseworthy, the experience that has been with the work in cross subjects does not allow to have many hopes from this recommendation. It would be more advantageous that the Ministry was taking care of abolishing the chapter of simple interest of the school books, and only was sanctioning the teaching of this subject like base for the work with compound interest, to imply never that the chapter of simple interest makes some sense when studied alone, as isolated subject, what has been taking place during centuries in the Latin America.

The idea of compound interest, which can Look like very arid and hard for many people, having there been even a group of politicians intending to prohibit his use, through law, is a consequence of the understanding that society has obtained of the currency functioning. When someone asks for you an amount as lending, at monthly interest, in the second month there is already an addition in interest on the original capital of the debt, and this addition is a credit, entrusted in the hand of the debtor, unless the payment in each month of the produced interest makes part of the agreement. If this interest continues there, with the debtor, has not been sense in dispensing him of the payment of this part of the debt amount, because, if he will be paying this monthly interest, you will be doing other profitable applications with this money, and, if you are not doing this, due to the absence of this capital in your hand, he, the debtor, is who is winning, since he wants.

The alternative to the use of the compound interest is the stipulation "ad hoc" of the remuneration for the rent of money during a determined term, thing that is not regulated whether by law whether by the market. This one is the system in force in the Islamic countries of theocratic regime. It is not anything that we should envy.

# Chapter 2. Gambling

Another situation in which the person can be deceived by the numbers is in the expense with games. The question is explained by a concept called of Mathematical Hope, also known like Mathematical Expectation, or simply "Expectancy". You risk an amount in the game many times. The calculation of the Expectancy shows the theoretical average of your profits. Suppose that you spend one year playing in the Mega-six. Then the average of profits in this year will be a loss, very near of the amount spent, being it able to be rounded up so that it is equal to what you have spent. The formula of the Expectancy is a sum of products, multiplications of the chances of winning by the values of the profits, positives or negatives. In each week, the Expectancy will be the probability of winning (approaching to zero), multiplied by the prize, more the probability of losing (approaching to 100%), multiplied by the investment done.

Let's take the game of the simple Six, in which the player will have to set right six numbers in total of 50. The number of different cards that is necessary to do to enclose all the possibilities is bigger than 15 millions. Then the probability of putting right the game with a card is one unity divided by that quantity. It is something that is frighteningly little.

The lottery game is, however, less harmful than those games that demand bigger participation of the player. Games like pack of cards, video-poker and bingo are those that more make addicted, because their results are immediate and frequent, on the contrary of those lotteries with weekly counting. Even so, if someone feels that is falling in a situation of vice for lottery games, he has to begin to do calculations and to think about the almost despicable chances of profit that these mechanisms offer. In case in that he doesn't dominate the processes of calculations wrapped there, he must look for a mathematician, or an economist, good expert of the subject, who shows to him his chances of reaching the "big luck". This professional adviser, mathematician or economist, cannot be a person who puts the faith above the scientific knowledge, which always depends on one healthy dose of skepticism.

*Remainder.* With information, how do I out of dependence?

The first point is to be conscious of that if the play supports a business, for example, a house of bingo, then it will guarantee much bigger profits to the owners of the house than to the clients. Unless there is a second branch - bar or hall of dance - coupled on the business of the game, the only profit that enters the house is the difference guaranteed in balance on behalf of the owners. Suppose that these want to be very just and arm the system of a way to give equal chances to them and to their clients. If they will give you equal chances to which they have, then in a week they will be able to pay the rents and to guarantee the salary of the employees and in the next week this difference will be in your favor and the costs of the business will not be paid. The only way of avoiding this risk is to arm the game of a way to give chances of profit much bigger to the organizer.

Think about a game with very small investment, like the one in which the owner mounts a table in the public place and shows three little shells under one of which he will hide a little ball. The player will have to say under which little shell this little ball is. Supposing that the owner of the game is absolutely honest in the fulfillment of the rules (forgetting that he was already dishonest while mounting this bench in the square), then the probability of putting right the shell is of one in three, while this of making a mistake is of two in three, i.e., in each throwing he has 66.67% of chance to win, against 33.33% of chance so that the profit is yours. Let's see the Mathematical Expectation. Suppose that you bet 15 monetary unities - he also marries 15.00 -. Then your Hope will be: a third multiplied by 15 (profit) more two thirds times -15 (loss), what gives 5.00 plus -10.00. This means that your Expectancy in the only throwing is of -5.00, or loss of 5.00. The set would be "they by them" if the owner was marrying the double of what the player invested, 30.00, since the probability of wining is the double. In this case, your Expectancy would be one-third multiplied by 30.00 more two-thirds times -15.00, which would turn in zero. But only a very silly man would buy a table and would carry it to a square to do fair play for the side of the circumstantial player.

*Equilibrium.* How about if there is no investment in one side?

If you are already convinced that the game that has an owner in one of the sides is damaging to the rash man who appears like a customer (it should be said on behalf of the owner that he is offering an amusement for a client, who must pay for this), it remains the situation in which two players are on an equal footing - for example, catching a lent pack of cards of a third one - and the game is carried out with equal probabilities for two sides. But hardly this is the type of game that compromises the economy of a citizen. If he loses systematically for incompetence, it is an hour of looking backwards and to be convinced that it does not make sense to him to keep on playing this fool's part. If he plays better than the other, he will gain much more often and the other is who will have to take this conscience. If the two play in the same level, there is no problem, except the loss of time.

# Chapter 3. Advertising

Not only the high interest and the games corrode the economy of the fewer prepared ones. The mere appeal of the products themselves in the market can do this if the citizen has no training of economics. And it is not sufficient to indoctrinate the own wishes, but also the wills of children, on whom the massive advertising in the environments of electronic communication shoot all the batteries.

It is the appeal of the advertising what does the client to buy a product that he will reject next. The disappointment post-purchasing has a pompous name, little suitable with the meaning, but that is the usual expression in the academic sectors: "cognitive dissonance". The objective of the advertisement is to convince the potential buyer of the advantages that he will have by acquiring the product, but the rash customer can imagine himself beneficiary of advantages that will not be a reality, in absolute. Some persons buy computers, bewitched with what they hear and see on the use of the device, but they have, as soon as they begin to use it, an attitude of incorrigible scorn for the machine. For avoiding useless expenses in this case, it is enough for the claimant to owner of the computer to make a course of one or two months to learn to manipulate it and to test his compatibility with him.

A necessary and important exercise to be done is to try theoretically the use of the commodity that the person is intended to buy. If it will be necessary the practical experience, then it must be done. For example, it is not necessary to buy a bicycle without being able to ride it. If the child asks to the father to buy one, the father must do so that the child first learns to ride bicycle, so the fact can be that the real contact with the product takes away the enchantment, leading the child to lose the will of acquiring it. If you are going to buy new clothes, it is necessary to imagine you put on it, to see if you feel well. This can be done by almost all the usual products that are intended to buy. It is clear that, if you have interminable resources, you can buy anything, without preoccupations with the "cognitive dissonance". But it is not this case that we are approaching here.

The mistake contrary to that of the squandering is this of the total avariciousness. Punishing the body itself and the spirit itself only to guard money is not a virtue. The four cardinal virtues, according to Aristotle, based in Plato, are Justice, Prudence, Fortitude and

Temperance (mnemonic: "Jusprufortem") and it is just this last that refers to our relation with the money: doing neither spend nor save any more than the reasonable thing.

*Superfluous.* Always should I reject spending on superfluous?

There is doubt on if a perfume is a superfluous good. It depends on something. It can be superfluous for a person and can be an essential thing for other one. A book called "*The Fable of the Bees*", which circulated in England and it is very commented by John Maynard Keynes in his principal book, "*General Theory*", tries to ridicule the campaign for the desertion of the purchasing of goods understood like superfluous. The result of such politics is the economical downfall, once substantial part of the productive activity of a country revolves around goods that are not essential at all to the human life. Great volumes of wealth are transacted in business concerning to valuable paintings, to most expensive rings of diamonds or to luxurious automobiles that cost twenty times more than a popular car. Abolishing this business would mean to launch the Internal Gross Product of the country in a situation of poverty. The unemployment would reach alarming proportions, even more if the measure includes prohibition of the traditional houses of games and show business normally incorporated to the culture of the population.

We know that for living is not necessary to us to satisfy only the physiologic basic necessities. Citizens need activities of culture, leisure and information. They need to develop affectionate knots and to nourish hopes. In the decisions on the use of these pleasures that are over there of the purely animal necessities, it enters the component of the luxury degree that is desired. Great luxury can be only responding to a necessity of showing a status not in keeping with the type of life of the person. But luxury and vanity are not a capital sin, once lust, which comes from luxury and many people judge vanity, refers, in religious terms, to sexual abuse. The luxury that deserves condemnation is what fits in the notion of pride, not of the use of good products. The sector of publicity and advertisement does not need to have itching when it does campaign for the healthy luxury.

*Value.* Are the essential and basic goods more expensive?

The formulator of the modern economical doctrine, Adam Smith, based his conclusions in what he used to call of Theory of Value. By this theory of Adam Smith, goods have necessarily two valuable forms, which are the "value in use" and the "value in exchange". The relevant discussion is that the value in exchange, expressed through the price, has not high correlation with the value in use, having, very often, negative correlation. He gives like example two products in which this reality is more obvious: the water, with very high value in use, but little value in exchange, and the diamond, of very low value in use and immense value in exchange. Normally, what gives this enormous price for goods with very little usefulness is anything that we might call of a value in "status", connected to the value of use. It is to say that the use is practically unnecessary, but it gives a high egoistic comfort to the owner of the good. This takes place not only with an expensive jewel, but also with a celebrated painting or with a luxurious car. Many persons acquire the product and guard it, not because they feel a such "egoistic comfort", whose measure would be the value in "status", but because they act "in Rome, as the Romans do", i. e., once that good has high value of market, having it is a good way of guaranteeing a reserve of value, a "hedge".

# Chapter 4. Vices

When dependence is a vice, the weight of the social criticism on the individual is much bigger than regarding any other dependence. Everyone knows that only a great dose of willpower will be a medicine to rid the person of this situation. Nobody freely will leave a vice. This willpower depends on motivation and this one must be fed by some objective.

*Tobacco.* Besides diseases, does smoking bring other losses?

The vice of smoking is still the most disseminated one and the conscience on the dangers of tobacco appeared in harmony with the advent of the ecological conscience. In the 18th century, Emperor Peter I of Russia, Peter the Great, after having learnt the habit in the times in what he lived in Holland, sworn in the Russian throne obliged his counselors to learn to smoke, because he was thinking that this was making part of the presentation of the civilized man. In the third quarter of the 20th century this conception was altered. A man dependent of tobacco started to give off the air of a weak man, who does not manage to dominate a vice that is ugly, pollutant of environments, incinerator of capital and damaging to the health. Already in the last quarter of the 20th century, the habit of smoking started to be an indicative of that the person is not a leadership. The smoke indicates a dependent person, so, not a leader. A chief can smoke, a leader, not.

It is by its past of sophistication that the habit of smoking was consolidated as the more ingenuous of the vices. Though the pain in the lung and the difficulty of breathing, at certain moments, reach all the dependents of the tobacco, it is only after centuries that the conscience of the damage that this habit brought to the health was made disseminated.

If it is to substitute the tendency to smoke cannabis, opium, crack or other more weighed drug, certainly the tobacco is still recommendable. It is possible to live up to an age superior to 80 years smoking 40 cigarettes of tobacco daily, whereas with this quantity of cigarettes of cannabis the user would survive only some weeks, when very much. Obviously, this would be the unique justification for the use of the tobacco, once the lung of a smoker is a very sad piece to be seen.

When someone quits smoking, this person needs to wait some months until the nicotine is expelled of his body. Then, gradually the fact is that he is realizing the changes provoked by the decision, when one of the most important is the sensibility at the savor of the foods. Who smokes more than ten cigarettes daily loses the chance of savoring a simple pepper, when not a chocolate or an omelet of cheese. The taste is damaged in at least 50% of its capacities. Like a former smoker, the individual discovers, as if it was the first time, the inviting and irresistible taste of the foods of his preference, and that he was not even noticed before.

Many people return to the cigarette because of this phenomenon. They are felt incompetent of holding to gluttony and, to stop putting on weight, return to the tobacco, which works like gastronomic anti-inductor. This is a proof that the person has not sufficient willpower to escape the tobacco dependence, so he was not able to stop and to deal with the subsequent consequences of the action, even this being a very positive consequence. It is necessary to have willpower for quitting smoking and regulating the appetite that appears then. The second control is easier than the first one.

Ten basic disadvantages of the smoker in comparison with other persons are presented here:

1 - He darkens the lung;
2 - He makes the pocket thin;
3 - He blocks veins;
4 - He yellows teeth;
5 - He reduces the taste;
6 - He is rejected like pollutant of environments;
7 - He burns clothes of the body and of bed;
8 - He loses the opportunity for leading;
9 - He stops cultivating the independence;
10 - He takes much coffee.

*Obesity*. If I am overweight, can I control this condition?

We accustomed, up to thirty-years-old, doing three daily meals, or, at least, having lunch and dinner. The body notices to be of use only of the necessary one to its maintenance and to dispense the rest. But for forty-years-old, the situation is begun to modify. The body learns to store energy, as prevention to a possible shortage. So, three daily meals, quite compound and quite enjoyed, can lead us to a continuous process of fattening that has not any more returns. For persons very inclined to put on weight, the food habit recommendable can start to be this of ingesting solid foods in a day and, the next day, ingesting only liquids, when alternating so, for example, liquids in three days of the week and solid in four days, or vice versa. Liquids can be juices, "detox" juices (without lemon), chocolates, teas, milk, broth and soups. Non-alcoholic beer also is very nourishing and, the experts in the subject say it, it is fattening only when accompanied by savories or other solid foods. He who did not manage to leave the fermented alcohol, or did not see reasons for this, this one can serve of alcoholic beer anyway. But pay attention: with alcohol or without it, beer is a compound of chemical substances that cause dependence. The pain in kidneys, felt by a great deal of them who took the drink for many years, can take place so much by the excess how much by the lack of the product.

Doctors recommend other strategies for them who have inclination to the obesity. One of the most recommended is always to continue with three daily meals, in the certain hour, but with substantial reduction of the volume to be ingested. This is a difficult way, which has taking many people to do the sad surgery of stomach, in order to reduce the size of the organ receiver of the swallowed foods. The fact is that feeling still the smell of the food it is not easy to stop in 400 milliliters when one is accustomed to eat 600 milliliters. It is better not to feel the aroma. Nevertheless, the problem can be resolved by rigid discipline.

Researches of the Clinic Hospital of Sao Paulo show that only 6% of the obese ones reached this condition for glandular problems. Others 94%, for much that it disappoints a big quantity of fat ones, they are besides the ideal weight for purely behavioral problems. For almost totality of the obese ones, there is no longer the excuse of that the problem is of metabolic dysfunction. But precisely there the hope must be: it is enough to change the attitude.

An obese is someone who is loading reserves of fat for wherever he wants to go. With this, one of the disadvantages is the tiredness that this brings. To climb slope walking starts to be a great sacrifice. When he dreams that he is flying, in this dream he flies with the belly almost trailing on the ground. The flight does not manage to take off, unless he is already absolutely adapted to the obesity.

But to be adapted by a situation that is not healthy is regrettable. Certainly, the obesity is neither a disease, but nor it is an ideal state. This does not justify the prejudice against the fat ones (nothing justifies prejudice, after all), principally because we don't know if the fat one who is at our front takes part of 6% of the victims of glandular problems. However, we know, at the same time, that the probability of this obese one to be in this condition for behavioral deficiency (sloppiness) is immense, of more than nine chances in ten.

Before the doctor orders, so, it is necessary to the obese one to have information on the counterbalancing of his diet. Very often the problem appears by mere lack of information. He must be supplied of cheese in the morning, in order that his voracious appetite comes to fall sleeping in the next meals. He must reduce drastically the ingestion of starches and carbohydrates, like rice, potato and derived of wheat, once they are vehicles for the transport of fat to the body. Solid candles with much starch, as well as the ice creams, are another great danger. Each adult person must discover his food standard with sights to the maintenance of the weight, as soon as the healthy body mass has been reached. For many people, the daily lunch will be enough, without ever having dinner, except in special opportunities. For others, the breakfast will be enough, with ingestion of liquids in the afternoon and at night. Others, still, take only the daily breakfast, but, like Don Quixote, have lunch once monthly. And a few others people, bearers of better bacteria in the belly, have lunch once for week. Citizens who, after their 35 years old, can have lunch and have dinner daily without increasing in slow and gradual form the physical diameter, those make part of a small minority.

*Fasting.* If I am overweight, must I keep regular daily meals?

The ancient practice of the fast, of ancient oriental and western religions, can be retaken through a new prism, this of the supportive fast. If great piece of the population to get two days weekly without ingesting solid foods, the price of these foods will fall in the market in first moment, and they will be more accessible to the persons of low purchasing power. Many people who try to fast give up then because go badly, suffer dizziness or thing of this type. But this is decided easily with the ingestion of fat, together with the liquids, or in prior form. For example, the milk must be with butter. In the preparation of the powdered milk the fat is withdrawn before, in the factory, and, then, he who comes to prepare milk from the powdered milk can add butter to it (before this, the integral milk is easily soluble when we mix sugar, or salt, before putting water; ingesting liquids with sugar is important to hold out the day of fast, but he who has hyperglycemia needs to look for other ways, and must use much tea of carqueja (Baccharis trimera), cinnamon and leaf of bauhinia forticata, known as "cow toe"). Besides the liquid butter, a little spoon of olive oil is sufficient to cover with grease the walls of the esophagus and of the stomach, preventing so the organism of leading the person to those sensations of ailment that many people suffer when they spend much time without eating. The liquid that must be avoided when the stomach is empty is the lemon soda, or some another juice done with very acid fruit.

With fast is nothing lost except a corporal mass? There is a cost, yes. In the following day after the fast, the person must avoid the sex, because he will have little enjoyment. The pleasure will not be compensatory. But, as well as the solid foods must not be diaries, either the sex will have to be. Another care must be with the breath: he who does fast only at the base of water keeps breath of whom is being gnawed on the inside, what is true, according to the demonstration done by Claude Bernard, that when proteins are not ingested the person extracts the proteins of the own body.

Those who resist to the idea of making an effort to grow thin must think firstly about the profits that the attitude of reducing the quantity and the frequency of the ingestion of foods brings. Accustoming to eat less leads to the reduction of the weight and also to the economy of time and money. The financial advantages are great. If the obese person changes his food habits and, for example, starts to have lunch only three times weekly, it will be left four hours of lunch, which will be dedicated to the leisure or to some useful work. The fast is also the best natural medicine against the high blood pressure.

Remembering, the cares in practice of the fast must be to:

1 - Abstain of solid food, from the awakening up to sleeping;

2 - Avoid lemon or lemon soda;

3 - Ingest liquids with sugar and liquids with fat;

4 - Limit the daily ingestion of liquids in 1.5 liters;

5 - Take care of the breath;

6 - Dispense the sexual practice the next day.

7 – Bring good feature, without downed air (religious advice).

*Index.* How to know if my weight is fit to my body type?

With a new food practice, appropriate to the maintenance of a healthy Body Mass Index (the index, Bmi, must vary between 18 and 25, and it is estimated by dividing the weight of the person, the mass m in kilograms, by the square of the height h, h in meters; who weighs 64 kg and sizes 1.60m, divides 64 by 1.60x1.60, i. e., 64 by 2.56, obtaining 25 as result, having in this case the superior limit of the healthy interval of the body mass). Children do meals three times a day and they use the substances withdrawn of the foods and added to the body to continue their process of growth. The forty-years-old ones who do full meals three times a day, grow for the sides, logarithmically, unless they are of that privileged few ones who have internal mechanism of elimination for excess fats.

*Alcohol.* Is taking distillates less harmful than smoking?

Though the obesity is not a vice (vice: opposite of virtue), it was treated shortly afterwards of the tobaccoism because of the connection that it has with that problem. Let's turn them our lantern on another vice provoked by lawful drug, the alcoholism.

The tobacco addiction suffered an excessive pursuit in the last times, receiving a much bigger load of attacks than the alcoholism, when this is a more harmful vice. This is, however, a mere historical circumstance. What takes place is that the attack to the alcohol in the first half of the 20th century was incomparably heavier than the thrown against the cigarette. And the shot backfired, almost literally. It was the period of the famous "dry law", in the United States. The prohibition to the commerce of the alcohol led to the clandestine market of the drink and to the brutish enrichment of the gangsters, the only ones who were risked negotiating with the commodity. The worst is that the attractiveness of the "prohibited element" led, for reverse effect, to the dissemination of the alcoholism, not to its reduction, as it was intended

This negative experience did so that the governments started to attack the problem of drink only with campaigns of recommendation, or prohibition of sale in the retail trade for juveniles.

When one decided to intensify the struggle against the tobaccoism, nobody cogitated on prohibiting the sale of cigarettes, what did so that the campaign had effect much more positive than the "dry law". But there are other aspects. While the smoke is something fussy, the alcohol is, socially, much more discreet, though it has turned out to be much more harmful for the health of the user and for his family. In the restaurant, if there is a citizen drinking whisky and, some meters over there, there is another smoking, it is the smell of the smoke of the last one that bothers the presents, not this of the whisky. Besides, the one who enters in the restaurant, sees the smoke, does not see the whisky. The cigarette loses for the alcohol in the nuisance to the sense of smell and to the sense of the vision.

However, hardly the cigarette makes the citizen to lose the job that he already has. Hardly the smoker is expelled of his house by the wife only because of being a smoker. So these two disgraces are great common among the alcoholics: loss of the job and loss of the familiar acquaintanceship. These two losses lead to a fourth tragedy: the begging (the first tragedy was the entry to the vice of the drink).

A fifth intermediary tragedy makes part of the life of he who handed to the alcoholism and this one should be most spread: the loss of the sexual appetite. It is not a question of impotence, what deludes the drinker, but of sensation loss. As well as the smoker damages his taste, the alcoholic damages his sexual performance because of reducing the sensation of the sex. And everybody knows that the sense of the sex life is in the sensuality, much more than in the mechanical action.

Besides losing the sexual sensibility, the alcoholic starts to present the incorrigible and insatiable affectionate lack. These two effects, lack emotional and loss of sexual desire, are shown during the redraws, though the first effect is already made present in the same day of the drunkenness.

It is very difficult to us to know what weighs more in the expulsion that the wife promotes against the alcoholic husband, if the loss of sexual appetite, the lack emotional or the loss of the job.

The incipient drinkers have to think always about the final tragedy like something dark: even when living in the gutter, begging for drinking, the alcoholic feels incompetently of exchanging the drink by the turn to the job, to the cleanliness and to the familiar life. The fact is that the capacity of taking conscience was left behind. The more the citizen is invaded by the dependence of the alcohol, the less he will be able to take some positive decision for his life.

Up to reaching this situation of almost impossibility of return, the belief of the alcoholic is that he is not dependent. Even when he is expelled from home, he still considers himself one no-dependent of alcohol. Now, it is not dependent only he who takes a dose of alcohol once each semester, at most, and never depended on the drink. Obviously, he who never experimented it, also he is not dependent.

The customary weekends drinkers are, so, the main candidates to vacancy of pathological dependents.

The Islamic countries prohibit the marketing of alcoholic drinks. It is an advantage in relation to the rest of the world. In the countries of Christian culture, the invention of the distillates in 1498 (year of the first distillation of whisky in England) could have unleashed the understanding that the custom of being intoxicating would change of nature in this time. But such a thing did not happen. Some Protestant churches prohibited alcoholic drinks of any type among their loyal ones, but this was insufficient to influence the western culture. The difference of lethality of wine and beer in comparison with the distillate is, mutatis mutandis, this one existent between the penknife and the machine gun. There would have been a great change if the Vatican had taken providence, if the cardinals had taken conscience of the destructive power of the distillate in front of the society of the Christian people. Once that this did not take place, and there is not seen perspective of that it will take place in the near times, there keeps on being this great loss for the people "of the cross", in comparison with the people of the crescent.

Once the current church has not any more secular power, it is of the governments that we should demand providences. And, like the experience showed, the total prohibition of the distillates produces a situation more disastrous than this in force today. So, it is the restriction to the market of the distilled, not the prohibition, what needs to take place. A first step can be the prohibition of the sale in retail, in bars, restaurants and kiosks. This works so that this poison has its access hindered, and not forbidden. He who will want to drink whisky or brandy, will need to buy the full bottle, in the supermarket, and will not have a table of bar to welcome the drunkenness. Bars will lose a little of the profit, since they will sell the fermented drinks, but not distillates. In compensation, the owner of the bar will not need to throw water in the drunk to expel him in the midnight. Other forms of making difficult the commerce of distillates can and must always be tried, under the preoccupation of that it is not necessary to reach the total prohibition. For example, if the person will not want to prohibit for all the clients' types the distillate sold in doses, the sale gets prohibited for more than 21 years old, being shown so that only to whom still have not the age of the responsibility is allowed openly the purchase of this product, to imply that drinking distillate is a thing of big boys, not of adult citizens. Furthermore, the destruction of the vital organs, with the consequence of announced death, usually takes place to they whom reach 27 years old, drinking from the adolescence. If the limit will be established in 21 years old, there will not be sequel in the body of the young person, and he will not approach to the phase of the unhealthy alcoholism. Before 1498, alcoholic drink was a food, once wine and beer were liquids used by many centuries to accompany meals. After this date, with the invention of the distillate, the act of drinking started to be something isolated, with sense in itself. The person goes to the bar only, for example, to take a brandy, an act that leads, with its repetition, to the destruction of the liver, because the liquid ingested is a poison of slow action. And if it is quite clear that the distillate is a poison, it has not sense in the permission to bars and restaurants to market it in retail, in its balconies or on its tables, in doses measured in the glasses. In the reality, bars and restaurants never should sell distilled in no type of packing.

In order that is restored a society rid of the disease of alcoholism, it is due, with passing of time, to look for the turn of the ingestion of the fermented drinks only to accompany meals or for the moments of parties, taking of them the privilege of justifying the act of drinking by drinking, what appeared because of the distillate. It is so because the ingestion of great quantities of liquids in followed days is unhealthy. The recommendation that is necessary to ingest two liters of liquid daily was unfounded, and it is already being fought. More than five daily glasses of liquids in the body provoke excess of water in the organism, once hardly a quantity bigger than this is excreted of natural form. The excess is expelled by the body in the form of sweats, when possible, what is not good at all for the feet or the genitalia. It is this excess of water that leads many people to present frequently burns in the thighs. The morbid dropsy demands more than this, but an exaggerated and persistent quantity of water in the body does not distance a lot of a form of dropsy.

In advanced phase of alcoholism, the individual who tries to take care of his trouble must look attendance in the health system, so that the suitable medicines are administered to him, once the abrupt cut of the drink can lead him to death in some days, and the slow cut is something that demands a vigorous willpower. Obviously, he who is not so dependent to point of drinking distillates several times a day, being able to jump days without the ingestion of alcohol, he can staunch the drunkenness without problems. And the correct way of stopping with a vice is to leave radically the object of the wish.

As soon as the person accustoms without the drink, for example, after two months without to ingest it, we should understand as absolutely reckless to drink again. The motive is simple: the body is adapted to the new situation, and it closes itself to the possibility of being massacred again with the receiving of daily doses of the poison. There is no any more openness to the turn to the vice and, in great part of the times, insisting on the recovering is fatal. Even he is still lively, the individual will present more visible and worrying symptoms of his alcoholism, like it is the case of the trembling. This sensitivity also takes place before the cigarette, once many smokers who stop smoking develop strongly rejection to the nicotine, being attacked by nocturnal tachycardia when inhale the smoke of the cigarette of other persons in certain moment of the day.

Several disadvantages can be identified for the alcoholic individual, some of them already mentioned in the paragraphs above. Like in the case of the smoker, there is also here a relation of ten basic disadvantages:

1 - Solitude - He dawns with incorrigible affectionate lack;

2 - Desertion - The spouse does not stand the drunkenness and a day expels him;

3 - Anaesthesia - He loses the sensation of sex the next day;

4 - Losses - He spends very much without realizing, like in the games;

5 - Disarray - He suffers cerebral dysrhythmia and dyslalia;

6 - Illness - He weakens his liver and body, attracting diseases;

7 - Discredit - He loses the credibility;

8 - He should not drive, because of accidents;

9 - Unemployment - He has bigger chance to lose the job;

10 - Alienation - He gets vulnerable to the strokes.

*Semiology.* Are there signs to the coming of alcoholism?

If the common symptoms observed by the smoker concern, nearly always, to the functioning of the lungs, with difficulties in the breathing, pains in the chest and aspiration that is not completed, in the case of alcoholism, the most reached organ is the liver and the semiology appears in the skin, what begins to be whitish and to peel. This takes place first with the skin of the hand, what starts to go pop, and after some time it is that it reaches the remainder of the body skin. Not even all of the persons have this mechanism of alarm working with perfection. Therefore, it does not make sense waiting the hand to peel for beginning the preoccupation with the health shaken by alcohol.

It is well known in a certain district of Sao Paulo the case of a certain citizen, mister Silvio, who was already presenting these symptoms from skin, when he received to work together with him, in his small particular business, his son, who had been expelled of home by the wife. Being the drink now shared by both, the use increased and in a little time mister Silvio died. In this time the son already began to present those symptoms. And in more two months, he died also.

The lesson that is possible to take away from this tragedy is that a father has chance very little of diverting his son of the way of the vice if he himself has no willpower to escape.

*Insensitivity.* In alcoholism, is it good to have no symptoms?

It is important to remember ever that the absence of symptom does not bring any advantage to an individual who goes too far of vices. What works is the opposite of this. In the first months of the cigarette use, or the use of alcohol, it is very common to the person to feel dizziness. With the cigarette, it is something guaranteed in the first drag. With the time and with the custom, those symptoms disappear, i. e., the sensibility of the body, in front of strange elements that are attacking it, it disappears. Far from this to represent some profit, what is possible to understand here is that the bandit not more needs to break the door down to enter your home, because now he can already enter without doing no noise, once everything is completely relaxed. But the robberies continue, and now with more subtlety and more facilities for your enemy. Many people make fun of the persons who already have seen ghosts, finding that the fact of never having seen one represents superiority. Many people make fun of those who can see the halo of the lively beings, thinking that the incompetence of seeing this is what represents a guarantee of health. This author never saw the halo of anybody, but he does not doubt the one who says to have seen this, because the Kirlian photography came to show that it exists, not only in the animals, but also in the plants. No human being can have all of the capacities, but the person must not see as anything positive losing the already identified capacities, like it is the case of the sensibility to the alcohol. If a person drinks and feels dizziness during many months and, from an hour to another, he sees himself drinking very much without presenting this symptom, he must see this like cause of sadness, because he had just lost a power that his body detained.

*Coffee.* Can the habit of drinking coffee become addiction?

The most innocent vice of all is this of taking coffee. In the old times it was drunk reserved to hours at the end of the afternoon in English pubs. A time more, the wives, tired of waiting for the arrivals of their husbands, who more and more were stretching the time of amusement in those houses, they decided to buy the powder and to prepare the drink at home, so that their husbands not more were needing to spend in the bars. The idea worked. And the vice was brought from the street to home.

For great most of the users, the custom of taking coffee never comes causing dependence, in spite of being a daily habit. But a small percentage of human being develops an almost indissoluble connection with this drink. There are, for example, persons who are taken with migraine two hours after the lunch if next to it they do not ingest a cup of coffee.

In England a strange and rare disease was identified, in the 19th century, caused by the ingestion of coffee. A woman, dependent of the liquid, was keeping the more and more dark skin, up to dying because of the problem. The fear is that this would start to be a common disease and that it was only a first case of a series, but such a thing did not take place. The fact happened like a big and tragic strangeness.

Today, many studies point to properties of effects so much positive how much negative in the caffeine, the active substance of the coffee, of rest, present as component of the soft drinks like "cola". People know from the beginning of the custom of drinking it that it is stimulating and, in the sensitive persons, it provokes frequent insomnias. The chronic insomniacs are the persons for whom the habit of taking coffee is constituted in an unjustified torture. To stop using the coffee maybe is not a sufficient measure to bring the cure of the insomnia, but it is unquestionable that it reduces the incidence. A person who when takes coffee always has insomnia, after stopping the custom, will have insomnias very rare. But to the person whom has this problem and does not want to get without the pleasure of savoring the aromatic daily cup of coffee, there is today in shops the decaffeinated coffee to resolve the problem. It, as a matter of fact, even helps to bring the sleep more quickly.

*Narcotics*. Should we treat drug addicts, or leave them at will?

Besides the three most usual lawful drugs, alcohol, coffee and tobacco, there is a number much bigger of prohibited drugs, because of having effect more accented on the health or the behavior. The pressure for the liberation of the commerce of the less harmful drugs is unjustified, so that he who looks for them because of not being satisfied with the lawful ones, certainly will look for a worse thing if, for example, the cannabis will be released completely.

Also the liberation of some places, as it took place in certain European countries, carries the disadvantage of attracting for the free territory many more dependent people of those drugs than what is imagined from beginning. But the transactions "B2B" (business to business), among legalized producers and universities, hospitals and research centers, they are a necessity, once that does not make sense there to be an underground, unbeatable commerce, to which the access has been only by illegal means, unless it was something absolutely immoral, like the commerce of human organs for transplants. Since the public power needs the illicit drugs for research and treatment of dependents, and their existence is not anything more shocking than that of any another poison, what the governments must incorporate in their way of facing the problem of the drug trafficking is this official parallel economy. So, those who became dependents of the product will be able to have the support of the health system in their treatment, being released of the dependence of the illegal traders.

However, how can a person help his family to get rid of the drugs dependence? Yes, it is necessary to have willpower, but this cannot support on anything. An important popular Brazilian composer has a mighty recipe: finding of maturity. The user should reach the conscience that he is not more childish to keep on being led by others who imagine themselves wiser. It is a fact that is implicit in this reasoning that vices are irresistible for the rebelliousness of adolescents. From there, to the adult society, principally to the government, it suits to make difficult the access of kids to the destructive drugs. Up to some decades ago, the difficulty was to get tobacco, the "cigarettes with filter". Smoking cigarettes was a display of resistance and pseudo-independence. In beginning of the 21st century, the cigarettes started to be highly accessible and, then, the attractive search of risk was addressed to the cannabis. Then, instead of saying "do not use this near to children", more productive is to preach "do not use this near to adults, who passed already of this phase". He who will want to look like adult and independent will have to rid of the drugs.

In this point, it is important to bear in mind that a small part of the drugs dependent persons represents a pathological case in the universe of the users, persons who suffer of uncontrollable compulsion for the self-destruction, the impulse of death ("Thanatos"). These ones normally do not manage to get rid of drugs without clinical treatment and admission.

Like aggravating circumstance of the situation, the adolescents of the beginning of the third millennium, very much more than those of the last century and those of other times, they are very sure that their actions in the world have nothing to do with others, of whom they are not influenced, either influence. For authorities who deal with young persons, it is useless to wait from these that have this type of conscience, the conscience of the repercussion of the actions themselves and of the compromising passivity in front of the actions of others. When it is necessary to act to release the young persons of certain sieges, it is not possible to count with the consent of the probable beneficiaries of the measure. In their immense majority, they imagine themselves absolute persons. For example, an adolescent who tries the suicide today has full conviction that his attitude comes from his isolated will itself, independently on the behavior of his near ones, the conquest that he did not obtain, the vacancy that he did not get or the support that other ones did not gave him. Any psychologist, even the beginner, knows that nobody commits suicide because of being finding much loved, much supported and much understood (being discarded the possible cases of self-euthanasia of patients in state of unbearable suffering). But is not this what the immense majority of the current adolescents thinks. Looking for interning an adolescent dependent of drugs and waiting his understanding, so, is wanting too much.

And there are also the liberal adults who struggle to guarantee the right of self-destruction of individuals. Recently they rose a comic term with which they accuse the authorities who try to interfere in the life of thousands of dependents of drugs who are accumulated in specific districts at the center of the great cities: they call these authorities "hygienists". Like those accusers see the drug addicts like garbage, they imagine that the one who looks for his compulsory admission are "sweeping" these persons from the streets, reason of that accusation. They do not admit that what takes place is that these authorities have opposite vision, which judges the dependent a person, with means of recuperation. If these "radical" liberals do not want that the dependents are taken to treatment, they want exactly that they perishes, by the continued use of the drug, and that soon somebody buries them as indigent. Then if they not see in them damaged current garbage, they see them like potential garbage. But, by the Freudian effect of the projection, they accuse of practicing "hygienist action" those who want to restore the human dignity of these dependents. Dr. Oswaldo Cruz and Dr. Drauzio Varela, in different centuries, suffered such attacks.

The law, as a matter of fact, presents difficulties to the compulsory admission of the dependents of drugs, on basis in the principle of freedom to come and go and in the principle of the autonomy of the person. But it is necessary to fight for a change of interpretation. If someone experienced certain heavy drug with the purpose of knowing it, then on him this interpretation that is done of the law is very valid, though it is not anything sensible to be doing experiences with heroin or other heavy drugs only to "know" it. But when a person damages his own health or starts to cause problems to his relatives once is dependent of use of illicit drug, even these whose illegality comes being much questioned, this person already lost the capacity of self-determination, on the contrary of what he usually says. The more he links to affirm that he is owner of his nose, more dependent and more ill he is. Just as he links to give in, warning that he has not any more conditions of taking decisions and needs help and treatment, then he began the way of the cure itself.

*Stealing.* Does a stolen object have the same value as before?

Among the apprentices of this type of crime, a small part of them does it for pathological impulse, the kleptomania. Other part, which people judge to be much bigger, does this for education deficiencies or for moral weakness. In these situations, the person will be already in the way of correcting his attitudes if he already gained conscience of the importance and necessity of the change. In the popular saying, "it is half the battle".

The first conscience is that the defense of the patrimony, by part of someone who already detains it, is one of the most exaggerated things that exist in society and it is completely disproportionate in relation to the meaning. Like an exercise, supposes a twenty-year-old individual, graduated in the high school. Only in the preparation of this boy an investment of at least 1,500 grams of gold is applied. Now, imagine this boy stealing a clock for five dollars of another citizen in the public square. Because of this, someone gives a shot in the thief and kills him. How many persons thereabouts do not die for a clock that seems expensive without being? In another case, an engineer, whose graduation costs several kilograms of gold, dies because of resisting a thief who wants to steal his cell phone of eighty dollars (next to six grams of gold). What a disproportion between the value of the engineer life and the value of that patrimony!

This attachment, which does so that the increase in value of the patrimony is very superior to the exchange value of the good open to question, has a psychological background very well consolidated in people and all of the historical attempts of defeating it were practically in vain. The most well known was that of the primitive Christian community directed by apostle Peter, in which there was no particular property of any good except the clothes themselves - there was not still toothbrush. That practice, as we know well, was not incorporated in the Christian society of the next generations, remaining, though, a detachment that we would not have without that radical experience of our ancestors.

From there, the first information that must be introjected by the individual who is a victim of the custom of stealing is this that the object that for him has at the right moment of the theft a value $y$, for his owner it has psychological value $y$ raised to the power 10 - not $y$ times 10, but $y$ multiplied for itself 10 times -, for example.

When the "friend of another property" thinks of "stealing the bicycle of that boy", he first must have in account that for him, who is not an owner, that is a simple bicycle, but to the boy, the owner, it has the value of an absolutely new Mitsubishi car.

Another aspect is this one of the upset caused by the addict in theft. In a school of thousand pupils a person appears from time to time with this type of problem. He steals a wallet here, a book there, a cell phone over there. The impression that the school community has is that there are tens crooks circulating for the corridors, when in fact he is only a person.

Two emblematic cases took place in a very peaceful school of secondary education of Sao Paulo where two thousand pupils were studying. A girl began, suddenly, to steal objects and money of her colleagues. After great investigation, the colleagues themselves arrived to a name. It was not necessary to call the person and to give any reprimand, once that for the solution of the problem was enough the community to make clear that already knew who she was and it was waiting only to catch it in the act so that a hard attitude came to be taken. The thefts stopped from that moment, showing that it was not an unhealthy case, which was demanding hospitalization.

Another case of that same school took place with the girlfriend of the son of a great famous businesswoman. It was a state school and this boyfriend was coming to catch this pupil in the end of the period with luxurious and varied cars, awakening envy and revolt in his rivals. They were several different cars in a same week. One day they discovered that the girl, together with one of her colleagues, another girl, was practicing frequent thefts in the classrooms during the intervals of classes. Those almost seven hundred pupils of that period got into conflagration, in the attempt of lynching the girl. Only with a lot of skill by the teachers it was possible to save her, through a false bottom that the school had in that time, a door of bottoms that does not exist any more in the current days, and that was of the ignorance of the student body. It would have there been, without that, the first death for lynching in that school only for cause of some small value stolen here and there in the class intervals, by part of someone who the pupils were considering "an arrogant little bourgeois".

*Robbery*. Does the current prison system regenerate the thief?

When someone commits thefts, he hopes to be protected in the anonymity. It is an ashamed and prudent form of appropriation of somebody else goods. Who commits robberies, differently, already exceeded the phase of the discretion and faces now his victims in crime of present body, though very often with the covered face. The robber is someone who exchanged the religion of the apostle Paul for the "religion" of the Third Count of Shaftesbury ("*Investigation on the virtue*" - 1699) and decided to confront society playing with the life itself (the difference between those religions is that, in the first one, "it is necessary that this corruptible body covers itself of the incorruptibility", whereas, in the second one, in state of nature the man "is essentially good"; what represents the crash between the belief in the "wolf of the man" - who needs to be tamed - and the belief in the "noble savage" - who walks for the corruption). Certainly, some malicious person made this revolver with which he now practices robberies to reach the hands of the potential robber. He who handed over the weapon is not, however, the society itself, neither that one who manufactured it. Thinking that society is this it is to confuse the callus with the foot.

The sadness for the apprentice of robbery is that he, in the situation in which he arrived, is much more distant of the regeneration than the apprentice of thefts. But the confidence, the faith and the support of dear persons are the miraculous medicine for the change of behavior. The counterpart by part of the regenerating is the consideration and the respect by those persons.

Unfortunately, the current prison, which does neither offer job nor opportunity for improvement of behavior, leads the detainee to the apprenticeship of more misconduct. Since the penalty of imprisonment for life was abolished in Brazil, in 1977, was implicit the necessity of recuperation of the prisoner, because he theoretically returns to the familiarity of society, in regime of freedom. But little was done in this line and the most well-known case of regeneration absence is that of John Acacio, the famous "Bandit of the Red Light", who was murdered in a fight a few weeks after being set free because of having carried out decades of seclusion. Another pathetic case took place in the Good Friday of 2005, in March 25, at the city of Franca, when a boy who was set free after having carried out his penalty returned to the jail two hours later, because of having committed two robberies in this small interval.

It should also be reviewed the dosimetry of sentences for assault. As the understanding of the justice in Brazil in recent years is that there should not be imprisonment for sentenced to less than four years, then convicted ones of assault must have increased their minimum sentence from two to five, or at least four and a half years, because the divulgation, very rapid, that petty thieves will not go to the jail made frighteningly growing the volume of theft crimes.

*Larceny.* Is it easy for a swindler to retrieve his image?

It is very sad to notice that the fraud is a practice promoted like a clear thing in the school seats, when the most of the schoolboys cheer deceiving the teacher, presenting as his production what does not pass of pillage. Larceny is defined as the act of deceiving someone looking to obtain advantage. So this advantage that the cheater or 'copier' pupils obtain in ephemeral way in each exam and in each task can indicate in the most of the cases not a future of financial strokes giving worrying to the police officer, but it forms, necessarily, an individual with dependent professional life, according to what was already demonstrated in researches of competent psychologists.

But among the effective swindlers hardly one will be found who should not have had his first training in the classroom. It will be a deeply regrettable case of romantic late transformation this of the citizen who has never deceived teachers and colleagues of school and has been transformed later in swindler. If did you practice school looting and, even so, you have become an honest citizen, worry so that your son is not a nectar thief in the classroom, because he cannot have the same luck that you had.

The individual who practices fraud is less exposed than he who steals and he who assaults and therefore his life of crimes usually lasts more time. The police officer is common to catch a person with more than fifty years old in this condition, whereas thief hardly arrives to thirty years old safe and sound. There is a bigger difficulty in promoting the improvement of the behavior of this individual because nearly always it is the case of an individual with a serious problem of nature, which would demand a solid moral education in the certain age. Impossible certainly it is not. Many citizens manage to apply some stroke of certain amount and from there they build a way of life, leaving the past of crimes and annexing the maturing to the conquest of an objective. If someone manages to start to show a good behavior after obtaining success in criminal act, with more reason this will be got of one who has not obtained any success, and has not lost the self-respect, which is made a great motive of complication. If the swindler is discovered, condemned, impoverished and slandered, then he will be in much more fragile condition for the regeneration than the one who maintained his image of good citizen without scratches.

*Stigma.* Is good measure to dirty the reputation of a criminal?

One of the traditional forms of punishing the criminal is to ridicule his reputation. Now, this is a very emotional and not much rational attitude, which does not receive the endorsement of the great Cesare Beccaria ("*On Crimes and Punishments*", 1764). The irremediable destruction of the reputation of the citizen is the worst contribution that it is possible to give to his chances of recuperation. This can have been the drama that destroyed John Acacio ("the bandit of the red light"), who even after three decades of seclusion continued to have his sad fame strongly fed, not only in the State of Sao Paulo, as in the country and abroad.

So, this naive wish of the condemned for appearing in the television and gaining fame for his stupid acts can mean the consolidation of his future disgrace. First because that condemned who reaches to be famous is one of the first ones to die in the hands of other prisoners when joined to them in the prison, so, far from affirming like leadership, he activates, in fact, much envy. And, second, his chance of rebuilding an image of worthy people is seriously damaged before the acquired renown.

For the society, the lesson to be learnt is that the bandit's famous creation for someone must be contemplated only like the form of denying to this one the possibility of recuperation. From there, if society does not want the regeneration of the thief what's-his-name, then his history, his name and his face must be spread widely in the television. However, if the objective of society will be different, it will be enough to inform that someone committed such crimes, without the spread of the identification of the wretch.

Even in case of the search of a fugitive, the spread of the name is counter-productive, because the pursued will use false both name and documents.

# Chapter 5. Self-destruction

*Suicide*. Where are the suicides?

The French investigator Émile Durkheim wrote in the 19th century a whole book on the suicide. By comparative statistical analysis, which today is done by the technique of the chi-square, he showed that the biggest incidence of suicide does not connect with poverty or anyone another type of trouble already incorporated in the daily life of persons, but with the change of "status". Suicides are more among the recently joined to some social group. He demonstrated also that the problem of the suicide reaches more the Protestants than the Catholics.

In this way, if someone is with suicidal tendencies, it is suitable to analyze first if the problem is not the adaptation to a new social situation. When the question is this, the approaching to the subject is easier.

The passage from the preadolescence up to the adult life is the most critical point, once at fifteen years old the young person has much less affection to life than somebody who is thirty years old, not only for difference of maturing, but also for lack of referential systems.

Many people imagine, erroneously, that the antidote against the suicide is the use of the pleasures that are within the reaching of the citizen. Certainly the pleasure will be an important component in dissuasion of the suicidal person, but it is not the whole thing, once that what maintains the young person alive, when it is not the religious belief, or the friendship, is the hope of better something in his life.

*Dissuasion.* What kind of pleasure can improve one's life?

If pleasures are important to talk out the suicidal person of his destructive intentions, it is necessary to know which among the twenty types of pleasure down have more effect on his psychism:

*Physiologic:*
1 - Nutritional (canapés / fruits / coockies / drinks)
2 - Excretory
3 - Affective (sex / fondness)

*Sensitive:*
4 - Olfactive (perfumes / roses / night jasmine / lavender...)
5 - Pictorial (photography / drawing / painting / video / TV)
6 - Musical (hearing / dancing)
7 - Humorous (anecdotes / cartoons)
8 - Hygienic (cleaning / bath / dressing table)
9 - Tourist (travel / ventures)
10 - Oneiric

*Relarional:*
11 - Purchasing (learning / gaining / buying)
12 - Ludic (playing / joke / sport / gymnastics)
13 - Friendly (talking / confidence / alliance)
14 - Telegraphic (phone call / e-mail / social network)
15 - Auxiliatory (solidarity / donation / incentive)
16 - Religious (worship / mass / prays)

*Intellectuals:*
17 - Education (teaching / catechizing / politicizing)
18 - Cathartic (histories / mood / drama / representation)
19 - Poetic (reading / recitation/versification)
20 - Logical (Mathematics / programming / computer)

*Pyramid.* Pleasures have equal value for different people?

The fact is that, in accordance with the famous Pyramid of Maslow, the necessities of satisfaction in the individual classify, from the base to the top, going of the physiologic demands, which are more basic, up to those of self-realization. In the scale above, the necessities are classified from the more physicists to the most intellectual ones.

It is necessary to take into account that this is a temporal scale, and not of socioeconomic level, like that of the Pyramid. So, for an adolescent, the physiologic necessities have a great weight in his life. For the most mature persons, the relational pleasures are more significant than the ordinary physiologic pleasures. And, when we presuppose that persons perfect themselves along of the life, the maturity leads the individual to privilege the intellectual pleasures. A twelve-year-old boy who reads the book "*Marilia of Dirceu*", by Tomas Antonio Gonzaga, practically wastes time with the reading, once he hardly takes advantages of the feeling and the formal great care that the author does to be visible. But a cultured person who has 35 or forty-years-old enjoys the poem like one of the great well written works of the Lusophone world, and, so, one of the great fountains of intellectual pleasure of that the person can dispose.

In the phase of maturity, in which the relational pleasures are the center of the preoccupations, many persons act putting their life itself at risk only to satisfy their necessities in question. Thinks of the case of that adolescent girl who was eating much chocolate, was not dispensing a packet of small potatoes and was also doing bulky meals. He was seen as plump by the colleagues, but she does not was preoccupying, because what more was still counting was the nourishing pleasure. Now this girl is 26-years-old and starts a struggle of despair driven to get thin. She passes days without eating, takes medicines supposedly miraculous and visits daily the pharmacy to weigh. What for her was fountain of pleasure, like the chocolate, now is a symbol of discomfort. She will be able to become thin, not as much as she would like, but she should reach part of her objective. After 55 or 60-years-old, however, the necessities will be different. Let's wish so that she cultivates her intellect, for then in the maturity she can enjoy the pleasures appropriate to the third age and, by daily exercise of the neuron, can avoid the progression of the Alzheimer's Disease.

*Self-depreciation.* How to avoid the young self depreciates?

For several negative circumstances in the life of the persons, or also for nature, a great part of them develop mechanisms of self-depreciation, and even of self-compunction, difficult to be overcome.

In certain cases, the delivery to the drugs, to the prostitution or to the begging has as precedent the formation of one of those mechanisms. The education system must look for that the pupils never lose the self-respect. On the contrary, it must stimulate in them the nourishing of the pride for their individual acts and for their qualities (this is not a matter of self-esteem). Developing a strong identity and a healthy individuality is an antidote against the "fall of the price" of the life itself in the future. For many people the own pride is built on the possession of goods, the financial success. But for the majority this is not the way of the happiness, when there is understanding of that "golden vanity" is more salutary and the satisfaction and the own pride are obtained from the conquest of the recognition and fro, the respect by part of the citizens with whom the person coexists.

*Shyness.* Can we cure shyness, or is it immutable personal trait?

It is not necessarily a case of self-destruction, but remaining shy can mean the destruction of the own career or the loss of great opportunities of professional success. Great part of the careers that can be chosen depends on treatment with the public and the incorrigible shy person, if he exists, is excluded beforehand of embracing any one of them.

It is not any form of shyness that needs to be fought, since very often it is part of a modest and respectful personality. The shyness that we should understand like morbid and that must be cured is this that damages the individual in his work and in his social familiarity.

An important lesson of the ancient manuals to put an end to the shyness is the recommendation of having not by heart sentences to be said. If you have a job interview, for example, you have never, beforehand, to decorate sentences that would be answers to possible questions of an interviewer, by the simple fact that a change of course in the conversation would confuse you. You should prepare, this yes, answers to inevitable questions, but not with sentences maintained by heart, which are easily perceptible for the interlocutor. If they realize lack of spontaneity in what you speak, then you will be lost.

Another mighty resource, in case of having an arrogant interlocutor and with air of superiority, is to imagine him without clothes. If this is little, imagine him doing physiologic necessities, an act that equals everybody in his animal condition.

The person to look at the ground while fails or listens is a regrettable habit of the shy one. Here it is the lesson that the problem is not the shyness, but its demonstration. A shy person has, so, to learn to hold how if he did not have this problem. Looking at the eyes of the interlocutor, not fixedly, but with naturalness, it is a "proof" that you are not shy.

Speaking in public is the great fear. So the shy person can be going very well if he follows some recommendations. Fixing persons individually in the middle of the public is only recommendable for the one who already has good skill of the technique of conference. The beginner, who must not look down, not to stare only at the paper to be read, must face the public "like a whole". Everybody will feel spells, but nobody will feel intimidated or, on the contrary, nobody will realize yours shyness, which will take place if you will look at that person whose approval you look for. If you are reading a text in public, lifts often the glance for the public, with care not to lose the line that is being read. This, obviously, depends on training.

General comments in the beginning of the phrase can serve "for breaking the ice". Examples: "I had a cold, then I apologize if my voice comes to fail", or "I caught a way with difficult traffic and for somewhat I do not lose the hour to arrive here".

Do not take a risk in pronouncing by heart any text if it is not very well memorized. If there is no security as for this, the best is to read the text. A certain graduating girl decided to say the text of the oath without looking at the paper, on the contrary of her colleagues of other groups. The others, who read, did the oath without any hitch, but she who decided to speak without taking the paper caused shame, once she forgot the speech simply in the middle of the oath. A colleague has come near of her and said to her softly the next word, saving her of a memorable hassle.

The specialized manuals bring other recommendations on how the person should to hold before the public during a conference. Besides the question of the glance, they speak also on the physical posture. Since there is the impression that it is uncomfortable to be stopped during the speech, many people try to relax, walking from a side to other, practically dancing in front of the microphone, or wandering, if the microphone is in the hand and not fixed in the pedestal. Though this is s resource to disguise the shyness, it is highly reprehensible, once it disperses the attention, which is transferred from the tenor of the speech to the physical performance. For many audiences, the steps of the panelist can call more the attention than the subject treated in the speech.

The shyness has the power of doing so that the panelist loses the voice during the speech. This obviously takes place with beginners, but it is a problem that can be avoided if the panelist takes care of using some stratagem that "breaks the ice". If the panelist realizes some difficulty in his emission of voice, he should, immediately, to go to someone in individual, someone who is at the side or, as a last resort, someone who is in the first line of the room. Certainly the person should not to treat of the outfit, the hairdo or any personal aspect of a listener, because this will make everybody bothered, but of a really general thing, like "I need a glass of water". It is thousand times preferable to disperse for a few seconds, in order to retake the breath, than to insist in a trajectory of failure.

*Neglecting.* Can I discipline myself to stop being sloppy?

The common form of self-destruction is the sloppiness. It appears in consequence of the mania of postponing everything or of the simple laziness. It can still result from a stranger mania, what is that of not be rid of the residues. A man of ninety and a few years, who died some years ago, he, because of having no relatives in Sao Paulo, had his house inspected by neighbors who would treat his funeral. The fright of the neighbors was immense while noting that the house was not having any cleaning by many years. The accumulation of garbage, the miasmas and the lard were implying that the residues were not turning out to be only of what was remaining of things of personal use at home, but that it existed reinforcement of mischievous junk from the outside, like boxes of cardboard, broken appliances, empty tins and other objects. There were also made stick arms that were like relics of his participation at the Civil War of 1932. It is certain that all of them were seeing that he was wearing the same clothes since an unknown time, but nobody could imagine the situation in which the interior of his house was.

Everything indicates that this situation happened from some manias in association with the Alzheimer Disease, illness that reaches everyone, in slow and exponential form, from the 25 years old, with more intensity on some persons and less intensity on others, beginning by the reduction of the capacity of memorizing, though a more conservative medical current continues believing in the sudden passage to the condition, among persons of advanced age. Then, all of the resources recommended by the medicine like prevention to those problems of the senility must be followed to the letter by they who should want to avoid a future similar with this one, principally by whom resides alone.

The necessary annual stock that the enterprises take in each December needs to be reproduced at home, individually. A good cleaning, with separation of usable and unserviceable objects, these last ones for discard, it must be done in this phase. And then to each day of the new year the person has not only to say, but, principally, to feel: "New year, new life!"

But, first of all, the daily cleanliness, in the clothes, in the ground, in the toilet, in the kitchen, in the mouth and in the body itself, it is an essential piece in the life. Also the physical exercises learnt in school, as well as the reading, are instruments to be used every day by all of the citizens. This is the biggest barrier against the invasion of the army of the senility.

The healthy habits do so that the person can dispense the willpower. For example, the oral daily hygiene is done by the custom. When the habit was automated, it would be necessary a great willpower to leave it, if this was the case.

For he who presents with theater, poetry or music, there are the own rules of each one of these activities, but the recommendation that is above any specific language is this of the training. If the text of the play is not very well memorized and gone over again, better it is to transform the presentation in a show of dramatic reading, the same thing taking place with the poetry. In case of music, many not much experienced professionals fall in the temptation of facing the public trusting in the training of one month before. The risk of fiasco will be immense. Like in the sport, it does not advance to train three following months and to stop one month before the departure. The training will be of eve. This is planning of the body and of the mind.

# Chapter 6. Dependence

Vices are, obviously, forms of dependence. But they are dependencies of things. Maybe you are trying to develop willpower to be independent of persons.

He who during much time has his life directed by somebody else sees blocked or reduced his potentialities of personal development. The whole regular education should, in theory, to be destined to the formation of an independent citizen, and not only a cultured and illustrated one. Therefore, the school has to, with urgency, turn his focus for the preparation of the individual enterprising, instead of an individual searching of job. If the person can undertake, with much more competence he will be able to be employed.

*Alms*. What makes a healthful person to beg?

He who has family and is handed to a beggar's life, what he is doing is enterprising to exchange the dependence to an identified person by an anonymous and adventurous dependence. This can represent a search of freedom in the humiliation. In the history of the beggar a case can be of deep disappointment with relatives, or even with a profession, like it was the case of a beggar who circulated in the traffic lights of the crossroads of the great avenues at Morumbi, Sao Paulo. Bended and of very long white beards, it was difficult to someone to realize that in other times he had been a competent and well-installed dentist.

Many cases of begging have behind some type of vice, but it is not necessary to have the pretension of mapping all of the ways that lead to this activity, which can be practiced by persons who were poor, who were rich, who were semi-illiterate or who were instructed. The more famous beggar of the history was Diogenes, of Sinope, who professed the cynical philosophy, as the first celebrated romantic. He thought that the persons must live a simple life, like that of the animals, exempted of any luxury and of any social convention.

Diogenes was not exactly a beggar, but a philosopher who decided to live how if he was a beggar, grasping a cask and putting rags on. A famous anecdote tells that Alexander of Macedon was with him certain time, when he seated in the sidewalk, sunbathing. Stand, in front of him and imagining that his problem was of economical lack, the emperor said to him: "Tell me what you want and I will give it to you". Diogenes answered: "Do not take me what you cannot give me", that was the light of the Sun. Ones tell also that he cultivated the possession of at least a good, what was a lantern, his lamp. He walked thereabouts with the lantern lighted in full light of the day. When someone asked what he was looking for with that lantern, he answered: "An honest man".

Many beggars justify their condition not in the Diogenes figure, but in the philosophy professed by him. It is the first practical manifestation of romanticism in history, if we can call practical something that has romantic background: "I wish nothing but to be able to live like the animals of nature". The ones who are more critical remove themselves of the interaction of their similar ones and become hermits, representing a sharp break from all human bonds according to their belief, because, for romantics, the human society is not a construction of individuals, but a datum of nature.

Whoever uses these philosophies to give forum of legitimacy to his anti-social actions, like terrorism, banditry, vandalism or begging, should take into account that at one time of adolescence his consciousness has undergone a subtle indoctrination that led him to the reversal of values now presented. For the first philosophical training we received from our parents and from the structure that surrounds them is the religion of our community. And both Christianity and the Eastern religions have their doctrinal basis founded on principles contrary to the romanticism: "The human society is construction of individuals, the natural tendencies converge to brutality and the person's effort to attain perfection must accompany him up to death".

Romanticism appears as balm for those afflicted by the consciousness of their little power to improve the behavior. It put the blame on society, which it says has been yet corrupted, and defines the individual as a mere victim, unable to overcome the destructive appeals that he sees around himself. Now, the very weak-minded ones are really influenced by the antisocial behavior and cannot avoid these traps. But when the individual begins to acquire willpower, ceases to be a weak-minded, or, if this is not the case, no longer will be susceptible. At this time, he must make so that the vicious siren song of the romantic ones echoes like a boomerang.

In recent times it has grown the stream of militant atheism, to the delight of the romantic ones. They campaign, both in analog and digital media, publish books and participate in debates where accuse opponents of being fools. We cannot confuse the militant atheism with the philosophical position of the classic atheist, because this one does not follow any religion, by the simple fact that he was not convinced that there is a deity, or even arrived on his own account to this conviction. He is correct in maintaining its position, although there is the dishonest atheist, who, by marrying a religious person, starts to behave as one of the lambs, practicing all the rites, without believing in anything. The classic atheist is like someone who does not think fun any basketball team and therefore does not have a favorite team, not involving with those who have one, whether to fight them, whether to defend them. The militant atheist, differently, is like the individual who does not have a team, and wants no one to have, because he thinks very damaging someone emotionally involved with a sports team. Like a new prophet, he thinks he's doing a great service to the world, attacking the followers of basketball teams like John the Baptist attacked sinners. And how does report those militant atheists? Using as a counterexample the results of the actions of their antipodes, which are the followers of the uncultivated religions (that are not the Greek, African or Amerindian mythologies). He handles, for example, the case of a religious fanatic follower of an ignorant phalanx founded for some whimsical, almost always a small proportion of a great religion. This fanatic commits a smashing attack on behalf of his phalanx, killing thousands of people. So the militant atheist out trumpeting that this act is the result of the existence of religion and of the fact that people believe in the existence of the divinity. In addition, while having never gone to prison to talk with inmates, this militant is sure that, if not all, at least the vast majority of these convicted is formed by religious people, because, he said, the atheist is "essentially good".

This militant atheism tends to incite an old trend among the Western artists and writers, from the Poles to the Americans of the West Coast, which is to deny their own religious formation. Invariably, these intellectuals are ashamed of their training (thinking that otherwise they would be confused with ecclesiastical preachers). This reverse effect, together with others that are identifiable and more harmful to society, denounces that Roman Catholicism and its Protestant branches mark these people with red-hot iron in the bud. He who wants a free position should search it in Leo Tolstoy or

Dostoyevsky, not in the authors of Western Europe, Africa or the Americas. The shame of the paternal religion by Western authors not necessarily puts them in the bin of the romanticism, but the naive attitude of unconscious militant atheists becomes the instrument of the romantics.

Armed with willpower and programmatic rejection of the romantic doctrine, the citizen will be able to escape those roads that make him to lose pride, friends, credibility and hope. There is a complication to overcome the abandonment of begging: the money. Both for those who play and for those who begs or steals or become prostitutes, a difficult component of defeat is the appeal of money with immediate liquidity. He who gets an employment and begins to work has to wait at least one month to see the color of payment (in the United States, a week). But he who begs or who wins the game gets the money right away. And when it comes to support an addiction, nothing more comfortable that immediate liquidity.

He who understands that money is to be mastered, not to be a domineering, this one is in the path of independence. This is not to take the command of the Hinayana Buddhism, of renunciation to any desire, but of valuing himself to the point of feeling that he is always above objects.

*Passion.* If passionate and despised, should I nourish hope?

Being rid of an unhealthy and damaging passion is something as necessary as complicated. More than in any other vice or dependence, the chemical alterations reach the brain of the person who is in love. Without counting the cases of physical damage, only the complete madness exceeds the level of mental damage provoked by passion.

The first step for the 'liberation' in front of a passion is the conscience that it is damaging. Then, the damaged must be prepared for a long path of four months, path that will only have effect if the victim gets in the absence of the object of passion.

A certain man was expelled of his house by the wife because of the alcoholism. A little time then she put another husband in order.

That previous husband, feeding hopes, but without managing to leave the alcohol, rented a house in the same street, in front of the woman house. For following years, he fed the suffering of being still fallen in love by the wife, while seeing her almost all the days, but being always rejected by her.

The vision of the person with whom the person falls in love is what feeds the brain in the production of substances that maintain the "limerence". After four months of distance, the brain gives up of directing the hormones for a useless waiting.

So the testosterone, masculine, depends on the oxytocin, feminine, to take to a man the sensation of being in love. There is a phase of induction, in which the testosterone imitates in many aspects the function of the oxytocin, for example, the inclination to the crying, if the woman open to question is a "crybaby".

The feeling itself of passion takes place by the induction of the oxytocin, not existing in his absence. A woman can fall in love with other one, but a man does not fall in love with anybody of the same sex. When a man considers himself in love with another, he has no experience of passion for woman and he has been simply devoting a great friendship for this companion. Passion is another thing, something that can take the victim, in very inflamed state, to the insane acts of suicide, war, madness, armed robbery or crime of passion, with the murder of the object of the unhealthy wish.

The commonest thing is passion to finish firstly in the woman, persisting in the man. When it ends in the man and continues in the woman, we have a situation more difficult to decide. It means that the woman developed a state of unusual dependence.

The advantage of the struggle for non-addictive front of a person in respect of the non-dependence in front of an object is that in the first case we can have a bilateral reinforcement. When there is dependence between two people and both want to get rid of it, the process nearly doubles its chances of success. If one wants to get rid of and the other does not, then the chance of release comes to a half.

The beginning is always shared, for more than one side may deny it, but the painful is that the end is not so. The one who knows a passion that has begun unilaterally, make sure he is in mistake. He confused idolatry with passion. Idolatry is necessarily one-sided; passion is necessarily bilateral.

The start of a passion only feeds with matching calls. A signal is sent and the response is received. If no response comes, the trying dies right there. This is not the use of the conscious intellect to interpret the gestures, but rather, the use of intuition and practical training. It is therefore easy to see when the positive response does not come.

Passion begins to develop within the individual when he realizes that the signs he received of the person are being denied. In desperation, he fights for attention, but the signs do not come back. In the course of this struggle, he realizes passionate.

The idea that the decisive hormonal role falls to women is not new. Clovis Lugon reports that in the Guarani Republic, which the Jesuit priests founded in the region of Rio Grande do Sul and Argentina, where now they are the ruins of the territory of the Missions, the decision about marriage fell to women. When a man wanted to get engaged to a girl, he said this to the Father, not her. The priest then called her and asked her to consider the proposal. If she accepted the request, returned after and told to the priest, who communicated it to the boy. If she did not accept, everything was like a confession, with the applicant involving not in any public disgrace, and certainly stopped feeding any pretension.

The strategy of the Missions priests avoided the occurrence of the game of saying-not-saying, responsible for many passionate tragedies. A negative by a young girl could even have power to lead the boy to suffer, but the process was resolved quickly for two reasons: the boy did not have why to continue feeding hopes and the situation did not come from a long time history. All he had to do from there was to forget the episode and point his aim to another girl of the community.

If the person has no willpower to overcome with style a passionate disappointment, even a marital separation, then he will be mortified, waiting naturally a new mood to visit him, which will take at least four months (there are women who feed the illusions of two suitors while the more advantageous situation do not qualify for her, and this will lead the future loser to a much longer that reasonable period of suffering). Being a willpower holder, the unsuccessful one will elect as a new goal of his life a superior phase in that a defeat of this kind will not be repeated. He is determined to prepare himself thereafter against a new fall based on the same ingenuity. He will take advantage of the event as a valuable learning.

The ones less likely to build their own independence may use this period as justified time of self-destruction and can surrender to alcoholism or attempts to conscious suicide.

The motor of the willpower is the pride, appreciation of his own personality, whether in glory, whether in defeat. It is necessary to believe that the ultimate defeat is the suicide itself and that hope of better days is the first way to victory. No ruler, no spouse, no boss can possess life and destiny of another person. In modern times, relations of human life are given through contracts, sometimes written, other times customary, and these are established as a partnership, one to one, one to many or many to many. And no partnership may include the property of the person because the person is priceless (the scheme of slavery, in which persons bought people, ended in 1962 when Saudi Arabia, last slavery country, abolished the system; we should not confuse, thus, bonded labor, which still exists today, with slave labor, unthinkable in the third millennium).

Staying with the one the person wants, when the other side has given up the idea, is therefore the hardest thing among all of the imaginable achievements. This is so because we cannot buy the will of the other, and the decision depends on not who is feeding the claim, but mainly on the concerned person. What one can buy from the other is the false acquiescence, and this is one of the reasons of nuisance for people who have lots of money. What is false and what is true in the feeling of those around you? You will not know, if you are always rich or powerful.

Thus, the strong will that we should have is not to get the attempt that was intended, but to give it up. Suppose your ex-girlfriend has changed your company by another because this one has better economic conditions. Also assumes she has made no secret of that reason. Then there will be for you two options: First, to enrich, for continuing trying to win her back, and second, to learn to live without her. Now, even if the first option leads to a quick success, a very unlikely thing, the knowing that she now accepted you because you are richer will lead you to respect her never as a worthy person. When she changed you by the richest, she was characterized as a literally alienated person, and this is not something that has back.

Of course, the learning from a great loss, or a big mistake, always brings personal enrichment to face similar issues in the future.

If you are in a situation of abandonment and passion, you need to cure yourself. Based on what scholars of the question recommend, what you have to do is to (mnemonic: *Aaerlica*):

1 – Avoid meetings with the PO (the Passion Object);
2 - Amuse with hobbies and mental work;
3 - Enroll items in the PO indicating non-reciprocity;
4 - Remember negative aspects of the PO;
5 - List your qualities that the PO does not value in you;
6 - Identify damage the PO brings in profession and learning;
7 - Confide with friends who support you;
8 - Associate the thought of the PO to unpleasant memories.

*Idolatry.* How can I escape the idol and the demagogue?

You can idolize a person or a thing, but neither action is recommended. The three religions arising of the Moses codes, Christianity, Judaism and Islam, prepare the faithful to reject the idea of worshiping objects, representations of false gods. This kind of idolatry reaches people who belong to a totemic religious phase, little higher than the state of animism. There is no reason to worry too much about it, so.

But the idolatry of a person, or many persons, in front of another person is something that is still a very serious problem in the human society.

As others have said, it is much easier to get rid of idolatry than of passion, because of being a one-sided relationship, what is to say, depends only on awareness on the part of the idolatrous. Of course, when it comes to a demagogue, he will do anything to keep captivating his followers and it falls to this one who wants to liberate see that he is being simply used for purpose of the malicious guide (strange is that in the early days of democracy, "demagogue" was just the elected head; Pericles was elected several times as "demagogue", the conductor of people; from then, the meaning of the word was becoming increasingly negative, because of the misuse made with the "position").

Long ago a Japanese rock singer, responsible for the wave of colored red hair, committed suicide. In the following days to the event, no less than 150 girls, fans of the boy, imitated his gesture. The parents of these girls, caught by surprise, certainly followed the course of the idolatry of his daughters, but could not imagine that the degree of dependence was at that level. If it were an idol of clay or wood that had been broken, the most that would happen would be a wave of juvenile crying. In the past, a war could spring, as happened in Mexico when, in the absence of the chief Hernan Cortez, who was absent of Mexico for a week trip, the soldiers destroyed the totems of the Aztecs, what was enough to break the harmony and friendship achieved by the skillful mastery of Cortez. Emperor Montezuma supported his people in the fight and Cortez, coming back, had to be on the side of his soldiers. Thus, the disgrace of the relationship between the Spanish and the Aztecs was sealed by the religious intolerance of low education people. Five centuries later, the spirit of the Cortez soldiers still is at large thereabout. Religious and political leaders must always be on alert.

Among worshiping a statue (or totem or golden calf), a living person and a person who has died, the last option is the least harmful and, in many cases, it is recommended. Idolize someone who has died is not even idolatry, but respect and veneration. A live guide can manipulate you, a dead one, not. Even you believe he's leading you, the option to follow him is yours, contrary to what happens under the influence of live people.

Some time after the death of a great public figure, his life is cleared in a balance sheet that shows the result of his contribution to humanity, whether positive or negative. Many deceive for decades or even centuries, when their contribution was made in the area of thought more than the actions. This is the case of Jean-Jacques Rousseau, mentor of several massacres, but still worshiped by a large proportion of politicians as a good person. Hitler has also, in this beginning of millennium, a list of followers that reaches 18% of the citizens. Thus, 82% reject him or are indifferent. This great opposition to his policy is due to the fact that he acted directly with a view to exterminate one people and dominate others.

Other leaders maintain the division of the opinion in a less clear mode. This is the case of Napoleon Bonaparte, who ruled with actions of notorious cruelty in relation to those who he elected as enemies, but he was who, by his intelligence and his ability, took the France of the crisis and raised the powerful nation position.

We should be idolizing Napoleon? This is not justified unless the idolatrous is also violent. You can admire him in what there is of positive in his politico-military operations, but should not cover your eyes for errors. Appreciating critically does not mean worship.

Already Pope John Paul II, the first pope to visit a mosque and a synagogue, has given, throughout life, unmistakable signs of his struggle for union of peoples and cultures. He was an example of peace and work. In the Christian Western world there is no reason to condemn idolatry to his person after his death, much less to the cult to his memory.

Protestants criticize the cult of saints from Catholic, arguing that Canonization is an election made by men in the Vatican, which would not have a mandate to decide who is and who is not holy. Now this election never imposed a saint against the demand of the faithful.

The Canonization is only the completion of a process, which recognizes as legitimate the worship devoted by followers to a given figure who is not alive yet.

Shinto, Japan's national religion, cultivates the memory of ancestors. The difference concerning to the saints of the Vatican is that the person does not depend on waiting for an election. There are bugs in this worship? It does not appear. It would be error if the idolatry were devoted to living, as was indeed the cult of the Emperor before World War II.

Those who still idolize live people contribute to the maintenance of humanity in retarded situation. Symptoms can be seen in followers of party leaders that act as flanges. He who has experience in political struggles know that certain acolytes start to talk with the accent and verbal tics of their chiefs. This means the gradual annulment of the personality in favor of the expression strength of the leader, like was denounced in 1548 by the French poet Etienne de La Boétie in the "*Discourse of voluntary servitude*".

The text of Etienne de La Boétie is the most important libel in the history written against the oppression of the political power, in just a dozen pages. The poet, friend of Montaigne, then was eighteen-years-old, but demonstrated a maturity of someone who has at least forty, and anticipated various aspects of the human mind that only five centuries after the Psychology would unveil.

Well over half of the world's problems will be solved when humanity rejects radically the lifelong or long-lived rulers. The president of France, for example, had very long term, until recently. Mitterrand, despite being a good person, could be re-elected to the position and remained no less than fourteen years as president of the French republic. It is an excessively long time, through which the head deforms the personality of less independent followers, while oppressing those who are not friendly. And this occurred in the homeland of La Boetie!

As society was invented from the observation of communities of bees and ants, there is a strong bias in favor of the monarchy by the simple people. When, in the April referendum, Brazilians rejected the return of the monarchy, they were, in reality, rejecting the power of the restoration of the Braganca family, not the power for life itself. For, a few years after Congress approved the status of presidential re-election, which was prohibited before, and there was not even a popular demonstration against the measure. In Peru, President Fujimori could not just be re-elected for a successive term, but also for more one, in which he was dismissed on charges of corruption. There was no public pressure against the election to the third term, but only against corruption, whose evidence was strong. In Argentina, President Menem asked the Supreme Court consideration of the possibility of a third term, with which he could turned fifteen years in office. The Supreme Court rejected his claim. The population most likely would have supported his new reelection if the case had gone to referendum. The worst thing is that during the period that should have been directed by his successor, four presidents were deposed amid the brutal economic crisis that set in the country, to the delight of Menem.

The invasion of Iraq by the military coalition led by the United States in 2003 happened precisely because of the indulgence of populations in front of lifelong dictators. If automatic harm caused by them were realized by all, there would be no dictator with support from anyone, but this is not what occurs. France and Germany led the campaign opposing the invasion, but suggested that they accepted the whimsical maintenance in power, where he was from 1967 when to this power he was hoisted as vice president. The deposits of weapons of mass destruction, the main argument used in favor of the invasion, were not found, but one reason is that much of the stock has been spent against Kurds, genocide that nobody can deny. The other part was certainly destroyed between the beginning of the period of skirmishes and the invasion itself. The son in law of the dictator revolted against his methods and, threatened, fled to Jordan. The dictator managed to convince him to return to Baghdad, securing him that he was forgiven and no grief was left in the heart of the old father. Returning to Baghdad, happy and comforted, he was immediately arrested and beheaded.

If there were, at least in the world said civilized, awareness and action against the Doom of dictators tenure, the US invasion would not have occurred, for the simple fact that the mentally ill Iraqi dictator would not have felt any support to his government. If he did not leave on his own, internal rebellion would have dropped him. This possibility did not exist because the blocking by the UN established years earlier was being sabotaged by many countries, including ones of the Latin America.

After the deceiver of the fall, the French President was pleased to emit note of clarifying that warned on the fact that the resistance to invasion didn't mean support for the dictatorial government of Iraq to the detriment of support for the US government. That later note came to the light because the French government realized that a considerable part of the population had understood the position of the government as of sympathy for bloody dictatorships. In Germany, neither the president nor the prime minister felt the need to do that clarification.

If the person, in good faith, makes distinctions, separating evil dictators of good dictators, concerning to lifelong leaders, then hardly he will rid of personal idolatries of what he is victim. The healthy attitude is to reject both as much the dictator for life as he who shows clear claims to be one of them.

If such a misfortune befalls on your country and you are not a mediocre person, to whom the national policy makes not the slightest jolt, then you have only two ways to go: to fight with all forces to overthrow the tyrant or to emigrate. The first option should depend on your level of engagement and the level of risk that you will be subjected. If there is little chance of preserving your life, so the decision to emigrate is the smartest, even because you can continue from exile the struggle by the removal of the misleading of poor who settled in the government palace of your country.

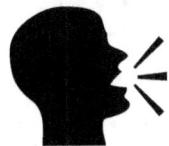

*Guru-pedagogue.* Should I follow or discard guru-pedagogue?

A form of idolatry that is unlikely to be seen like such a thing is that in which you follow the advice and guidance of a lifelong guru-pedagogue, while losing gradually the ability to take decision on your own. This person, who plays guide, feels comfortable in his position and is pleased to direct the lives of others. He sees, often unconsciously, other human beings as foals and dogs that should be tamed to satisfy always the will of the coach.

He is not like a slave master, who has an explicit relationship of command over his subordinates. The psychological power of the guru-pedagogue is subtle and often is not noticeable by third parties.

The resistance to the action of such a person should not mean that we should reject the guidance of wiser and more experienced people. A healthy relationship of admiration and respect for people we consider our guides should occur not directed at an individual, but to many. I can have a friend who advises me on partisan political issues, other who advises me about natural medicine, another who guides me about problems of exact sciences and also one who leads me in transcendental areas. None of them is my guru-pedagogue, because my base of knowledge has been formed from contributions of several masters.

The problem is configured as unhealthy when all my actions depend on the opinion of a single citizen, or when all of the other masters I have start to have the word minimized and questioned to the detriment of the pretension of truth to the word of only one.

If you have difficulty getting rid of the "intellectual" guardianship of a given guru-pedagogue, you must, first of all, consider that only a narrow-minded person intends to guide the other steps by long time. Any less obtuse individual struggles for mental liberation of his friends and sees any help needed as temporary and intended just to give conditions to the consequent autonomy.

Here there will be the temptation to think of Don Quixote as a possible example of guru-pedagogue. Yes, his faithful squire Sancho Panza had him as an absolute guide, but the rider, besides to be fiction figure, was crazy, what can be understood as another more message from the genius of Cervantes: one among the forms of madness is the need to control the decisions and the destiny of others. Think of another great Spanish, of real existence: El Cid or El Campeador, nicknames of Rodrigo Diaz de Bivar, hero of the Reconquest. Who was his faithful squire? He is not known. El Cid was a real hero and he was not crazy. He had friends and had commanded, but had not need to set aside the personality of any of his followers.

The elementary school, which comes from the "paideia" of ancient Greece, has a single teacher for each classroom. From the junior high level, for children as young as eleven, there is the multi-teaching school, in which the student has at least eight different teachers, dividing areas of knowledge. The significance of this is that from the beginning of adolescence, the individual must diversify his models of behavior to better compose his personality. So, the early choice of the career could bring the student to settle the orientation of only one teacher, despising others, and it should be discouraged. If the teenager has made clear to himself that he requires good knowledge in all areas, and also that he can change his mind later, so there is not great danger in choosing a future career as early as eleven or twelve, but the school should not encourage this by having not guarantee that the student will have such a clarity.

*Super-mother.* Mother is unique; so, is good to have supermom?

A dependence that is becoming increasingly common is this on the supermom. Certainly, this is a two-way street, because a mother who wants to see free her son (not who wants to get rid of the child) will not bore his girlfriends, doing everything for him to leave them and do not make any long-term project with any of them. The unhealthiest example of supermom is that lady whose son enters a college in another city and, immediately, she moves to the city to continue caring for her offspring.

Obviously, the traditional, more efficient and more effective way for the child to get rid of supermom dependence is the achievement of a job or some other means of support. While getting his own salary, the son who feels suffocated by maternal impositions may even without relocating and without marrying, rent a room pension, for example. With this he would be doing a great benefaction to him and to her.

Does it seem strange to have the family home and go live on board in the same neighborhood? Yes, but the break of the unhealthy dependence relationship justifies it. Much less justifiable is a 35 or forty-years-old boy to continue in "apron strings" of his mother, taking her his guru-pedagogue.

We should not interpret such attitudes as an attempt to diminish the respect and the affection the child must have by his parents. Never a mother will have dimension of what her child means for her if she does not spend a period of months, or even years, away from him. The reverse is absolutely true. As much as the son of supermom think know the emotional value of his mother, this value will only be really understood in long absence.

Nobody has to think that to take a year away from the mother will decrease the affection. A year away from a girl is enough to rid the endocrine glands of the hormone production directed to her, what may represent the end of the idyllic relationship. But the affective relationship from the son to his mother not only is eternal as it starts to have more and more sense over time.

Thus, paradoxically, getting rid of the supermom is to establish the necessary distance to usufruct her affection of a sound and lasting way. A cartoonist Ziraldo framework, presented years ago, shows rightly the meaning of the exaggerated and harmful supermom protection. The son is bound to travel by plane for the first time; then, concerned as always with the boy's life, she will ask the pilot, "Lord Commander, please fly slowly and softly, yes?"

If the captain had attended the will of the supermom, would be the first and last trip of that boy in the living world.

The comic is illustrative in many ways, one of which showing that supermom, correct in her exaggerated care, wrongs by letting not her son to act on his own, without nursery interference that, by poking her nose where it should not, can destroy the life of the protected, virtual or effectively.

Again, it is worthy the recommendation of Aristotle in his "*Nicomachean Ethics*": virtue is in the middle, the golden mean.

The affection and the mother's attachment to her child may not exceed the limit of common sense. The severity, needed to educate, should not also exceed a certain level of hardness, under risk of achieving the reverse effect, by the well-known "law of effect" (Edward Thorndike). The middle means there to temper gentleness with firmness. If the mother cannot by herself, the son must contribute toward achieving this balance. Who has true appreciation by the mother also has an obligation to close not his eyes to the defects that she presents and to try, with very way and with great skill, help her to correct them. The mother should not be seen as something sacred, which does not have where to improve. Seeing his mother's weaknesses is a way to understand her and love her even more. For someone who only knows his mother's strengths, without any weakness, this one develops a lot of respect and reverence, but hardly loves her like the person has to love a human being. Probably the easiest dependence to cure is this in relation to super-mother, but this largely depends on the protected son's willpower. He has to want to be free and must have awareness of this need. Otherwise, neither the first step will be taken.

*Fanaticism.* How can I rid my son to become fanatic?

The diverse background, and even more this that brings basic philosophical notions of the scientific treatment, such as Aristotle's recommendations on our inability to see beyond appearances, and of Descartes, who teaches us to doubt everything, is antidote against the youth entry in fanaticism, whether religious, whether political, the latter being a disguised version of that. But often the school and the family fail to ensure this training and see the disciple or son leaving to join hosts harmful to society.

So that the person gets rid of fanaticism, whether he is under possession of such a psychopathology, it is necessary to distinguish belief and faith. The belief is not the result of analysis, but free delivery. Hitler, a bad reader, was not a man of faith, but of belief. He read some pseudo-scientific texts and swallowed them as if they brought the clearest truth. In his *My Struggle* ("Mein Kampf") he wrote that persecuting Jews he was "doing the Lord's purposes." This was not result of faith, but of a belief, which can be anodyne, and that in some cases can be a source of tragedy. Faith, unlike belief, is not surrender, but a sound bet, a form of confidence. If we have two friends, one of weak character and other with great character, it is in this second that we place more confidence. We know that our assessment may be wrong, but our faith will go to him, not to that first, bit of character. If the first friend tells us given fact and his version is contrary to what is presented to us now by the other friend, it is in that last we tend to trust. Finally, the belief may be blind, not faith. "Blind faith" is only a strength expression. Suppose a devastating epidemic is affecting the population and is already close to your house. All estimations indicate that, if not contained, it will reach your family. If you have blind belief, you will pray and you will be sure with your prayers the epidemic will be contained. If you have faith, and will pray and tarry that if you are worthy, your house will be free, but you will never be absolutely sure that this epidemic will not come to your door.

A fanatic is willing to kill or die for a belief. His brain, if one day was sound, now suffers of a serious disorder. In the late twentieth century pharmacology developed powerful drugs against madness, something unthinkable decades before. Families should not hesitating to use these products, although they are not given in due form. Psychotropic d1rugs and antidepressants have been prescribed as if they were mere painkillers, medicine for somatic problems. Many clinical doctors earn incentives to indicate various products, without care to avoid dangerous mixtures. If a family has a crazy or fanatic young, it should medicate him, but should never mix medicines.

Certainly, providing medicines against madness to a young fanatic is a last resort, but this should be used when the person realizes that arguments do not make sense to him. One of the methods used in psychiatry to confirm a state of madness is loss of control of the logic axioms. It is in the case of fanaticism, and not in that crazy having outbreaks and promoting violence at specific times, that the test of logic is most effective. Bertrand Russell insisted that allied governments considered the Nazi leaders as lunatics, what would avoid greater carnage, but he was unsuccessful in this. Magda, the wife of Goebbels, when, realizing the defeat of Nazism, poisoned the children of the couple, she showed that she was dominated by blind belief, not by faith. The extreme fanaticism is therefore a contagious disease that can and should be cured with drugs and quarantine.

*Paranoia.* Is it healthy my son to believe in conspiracy theory?

Less harmful than fanaticism, but no less worthy of attention, is the case of the paranoia. In most of the time it is self-induced and, therefore, can be resolved with increased willpower. First, the person needs to be aware that he is a victim of the problem, or nothing will change.

When the person is in a stage in that the acts out of control, for example, punching someone without there being a plausible explanation, he came to the time to look for a clinical psychologist or a psychiatrist. But if the situation is just the difficulty of living together, by intolerance, panic, irritability in living or something like this, it is time to try to reverse the situation with the help of friends and with the own determination to improve.

Persecution mania, despotism, delusions of grandeur, inferiority complex and belief in the conspiracy "theory" are some of the ways in which the paranoia can entangle you. These things can be started because of a misinterpretation about some events, or some learning, which, with feedback, shall constitute an pathological picture.

Take the case of the conspiracy "theory", which must now be addressed directly as "paranoia of conspiracy", also so that the fact brings in its own naming a scarecrow, which destroys the aura of seriousness with which it usually comes to the mind of its victims. A "paranoia of conspiracy" carrier firmly believes in the "theory" that explains a given event in contrary way to that accepted by the press, and if anyone doubts his belief he presents very angry. A case in point is the overthrow of the Twin Towers in New York on September 11, 2001. The standard explanation for this is that suicide fanatics guided by Bin Laden, the Arab leader of Al Qaeda, destroyed the two buildings as retaliation for against the US policy for the Middle East. The paranoia of conspiracy has a simpler and more direct explanation: according to it, the fall of the Towers was caused by the US government, through the Pentagon, to be used as an excuse for an invasion of Arab oil-producing countries.

The development of this paranoia assumes a more basic belief that results from bad school education: rulers generally are able to Machiavellism so deep that Machiavelli himself would never have been able to imagine. This present author when a young man had a tendency to develop this neurosis. In a conversation with a professor of the University of Sao Paulo (USP) and other of the University of Campinas (Unicamp), was cautioned that, contrary to what young people think, rulers have no ability to weave Machiavellian plots that resemble the spectacular chess moves. They, at best, realize their craft everyday to govern. Even those who take Machiavelli as a Supreme guide limited themselves to areas already retained. Creative people are likely to cultivate this paranoia, imagining that the ruler has the same gifts that great fiction writers often present. This is what occurred with Professor John Nash (1928-2015), one of the great mathematicians of the twentieth century. In a mixture of persecution mania and paranoia of conspiracy, he believed that the Russian Secret Service, from the Soviet Union in that period, published mysterious codes in the Western press as messages to agents throughout the world. He surrendered to a desperate and lasting task to try to identify and decipher these codes. When the problem has reached the stage of

63

causing losses, material and human, he came under hospitalizations. Those hospitalizations themselves not healed him, but showed him that there was something wrong with his mental constructs. He then cured himself alone, by the awareness of the problem and the own willpower.

The history of Professor John Nash is emblematic. It teaches how many mental problems are self-induced and how they can be incinerated by their carrier. The ideal situation is that the victim does not wait so long, getting rid of the torment quickly, before it is installed in a dramatic form.

*Medicines.* Up to what extent are industrial drugs good mates?

It is known that many dependencies on people are changed by object dependencies. Many who boast of not falling into addiction to alcohol or tobacco, fall innocently in dependence on medicines. It is needless to be hypochondriac to develop this habit, which relies more on a credulity attitude or dazzle by the progress of science and technology.

It turns out that the basis of science is experimentation, and the truth, its goal. However, in many situations, what is imagined to be a scientific result is only a stage of experimentation. When in the Middle Ages doctors applied bleeding in patients for "purifying" the blood, it was used there a belief settled in the science stage of that time.

The first serious concept that must be incorporated by those who want to abuse the industrialized drugs is that their use implies side effects in nearly one hundred percent of the cases.

The drug-dependent takes a medicine to cure a particular disease and then immediately other symptoms appear, if not more than one. So he goes back to the pharmacy, armed or not with prescription, and gets a new medicine, maybe two. This routine will lead the dependent to a situation of voluntary servitude that will bring him more and more losses, in finances and health.

Conscious pharmacists gain from these vices, but are not satisfied with them. Ideal for pharmacy professional is to cure the disease he did not help to emerge.

If this problem plagues you, accustom to use natural medicines: teas, juices, vegetables with medicinal power and other products that hardly do harm to the user. Even so, be careful, because many foods can not be eaten daily, because the body needs two days for processing molecules. Some of these are: eggs, pepper, black pepper and chocolate. Eggs when are eaten daily are an almost safe source of thrushes. Other foods overused produce pimples, and so forth.

Drug-dependents are, for all purposes, drug addicts. Some can get the "mix" that will meet their chemical needs. Certain student who was hospitalized several times by use of drugs, with time became friends with the staff of the hospital pharmacy and hence could, during periods of hospitalization, produce and ingest doses of "medicines" that were true hallucinogenic cocktails.

This is one of the reasons that lead to strict control over the sale of medicines. If there were freedom to buy any medicine without a prescription, you can imagine what could be done.

For getting rid of dependence on drugs the most suitable way is to change the practice of intake of manufactured drugs by natural products, preferably diet dosage of healthy food and of acknowledged medical power. There is certainly no natural substitute for drugs like penicillin, for example. But these drugs without natural substitutes should be used on rare occasions, never systematically and customary, unless under strict medical monitoring.

A young woman who suddenly went to rely on drugs and inhalations against bronchial asthma attacks did not realize until she was advised that the emergence of the problem coincided with the time when his father, unemployed and separated from his wife, stepmother of this young, came to live in her home and, within that same house, smoked a pack of cigarettes per day, leaving the environment completely impregnated with nicotine and other pollutants contained in the smoke of tobacco. There, it was not the case to change the industrialized remedy by the natural one, but of cutting off the production of the disaster, which was the cigarette smoked inside the house. Since then, her father went to smoke on the stairs leading to the street, leaving the house airy.

Many dependencies of drugs therefore can be cured by simple removal of the disease that citizens think heal with industrialized remedies. But not always the thing is so simple, and you cannot always identify where the problem comes from. Therefore, the most convenient is to go even switching to natural treatments. For this there are many books in the place, various prices and sizes and multiple levels of quality and rigor. The person must be careful with quackery, once for medicating it is necessary to have recognized diploma, but to publish book, no.

So is that recently it has come on the market a book about healthy and medicinal eating. It is a work of fancy and attractive binding, with thousands of colors, with interior also very colorful and glossy paper. It was soon found that the medicinal recipes of the book are a fraud, what was already possible to see from the first advertisements. Do not let, therefore, impress yourself with the colorful figures and the brightness of the paper, because all of this can be intended only to deceive and yield profit, which does not mean that an expensive and graphically very well worked book cannot bring serious information.

*Machine.* Can depending on machines become a problem?

Dependence in front of machines is a very new phenomenon in the history, reason why we don't give much importance to it. It is known that already in the early eighties of the twentieth century some teenagers in South Korea died of cerebral seizure by spending too much time sitting in front of the computer unable to turn off the games. Until that time there was no examples of tragedies caused by dependence in front of the machine. From such cases is that parents started to be very careful with the hype of their children in the use of computers and video games, but this precaution does not prevent the emergence of unhealthy dependence.

Depending on his predisposition, a child who uses the computer for only an hour a day can develop this dependence. The most susceptible ones, it seems, are the least endowed intellectually, and that's something to prove. The less endowed is the child, the more he feels rewarded with the machine work, which appears to be thinking for him, and he will be increasingly "in its hands", like that faint of mind pieceworker who makes everything the head of gang orders. The other possibility, this very minority, is the boy who dominates early the machine handling processes and begins to like it as a racing driver likes his cars. But parents should not have illusion, because the computer is a machine with algebraic and logical operation of high sophistication, so that to master its working the young people must be familiar with at least the contents of the last year of the High School. Any eighth or ninth grade boy who surrenders to computer programming is being too early, putting the cart before the horse, and this is foolhardy when it comes to the development of mental abilities. There is a risk, because cases already were identified in this sense, with he coming to see his similar ones with little indulgence, telling them "you are not men, machines is what you are", a reversal of the memorable said from Charles Chaplin in "Modern Times". Anyway, there are many teachers and educational system leaders allowing and even recommending the use of electronic machines in classrooms of basic education. There are even those who, not happy by exchanging the multiplication table by electronic calculators, preach the end of cursive, arguing that only block letter is required today by being the letter used in mobile phones and tablets. Such people are heard and have many followers because the evils caused by the use of electronic devices by children are not clearly set.

Which equipments are healthy to educate small ones? Surely, they are those that they can disassemble and reassemble, without prejudice of seeing them functioning normally, as wooden carts, pulled, at most, by elastic or something so. Any instrument that relies on electronic circuits crashes when disassembled and reassembled, bringing frustration for the child, who will fell unable to interfere with devices the world presents him. In this sense, the filament lamp is educational, unlike fluorescent lamps, for in the Edison lamp the child sees the illuminated copper thread after switching the power and for understanding what is happening it is enough someone to explain, or he to read on the phenomenon of maintenance of electrical ignition in closed vacuum glass bulb, because the spark of the electric shock can be known and understood already in the first years of life. If the child move the lamp and allow air to enter the bulb, he will learn that the lamp no longer lights up, but this does not represent any frustration, because he knows that only with another machine he could remove the lamp air so that the filament does not burn, and that's what had to be done by any adult. There is not mystery in this process, unlike the operation of the computer, which depends on good knowledge of logic, functions and electronics, subjects that are far beyond the absorptive capacity of children or preteens.

In Portugal, yet before the end of the twentieth century children came to be required by schools to use calculators in examinations of Mathematics, what led to a very serious economic problem in the country between the years of 2010 and 2011. Will be it healthy, thus, preventing the child to know cell phones, electronics calculators and computers? None of this. This prohibition may have as harmful effects as to provide him free access. The child must know these instruments, but not to the point of owning them or spend hours daily manipulating them. As for the calculator, Pascal did not invent it for use in the classroom, but for professional use in finance, once his father, the recipient of the invention, was tax attorney.

For thirty years, from the mid-forties to the mid-seventies, adults knew about computers, saw them, but they could not touch them, unless they were technical, and it did not leave any adult with mental sequelae. For the child, the fact his friend to have a computer in the room table to play, see naked women in the Internet and talk in social networks, all of these things can cause envy, but it will last until the future results to show that the investment of that father who handed the computer to his son was something done wrong - if someone wants to make comparisons must take into account that the income power of the households must be equivalent in both cases, so that spurious correlations will not provide disparate conclusions. Yes, you will hear a defender of the machines to say his son grew up using electronic calculators and computers without affecting his mental development. But you must take into account some inconsistencies in that "conclusive" statement: (a) the case is only one person, who was not susceptible to the problem; (b) that parent has no way to compare his child with what he would be if he had not grown up surrounded by electronic machines; (c) if the child has developed some behavioral bias ("machines is what you are"), the person less able to see this is the father.

Anyway, people who do not see problems in the early use of electronic machines are more numerous among professionals of areas distant of technological than among the technicians. These, mostly, knows very well the danger, that delayed pump that is the "early intellectualization of the child", for using the expression of V. W. Setzer, founder of the Computer course at the University of Sao Paulo.

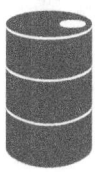

*Investment.* Are there techniques to learn to save and invest?

The opposite of the dependence, in a broad sense, is seen by many like the financial independence, the lifestyle in which a citizen reaches the end of the month, any month, without having spent all the income he has. This situation is achieved not when using the money to buy everything the person wants, but when he can save, make a investment in the bank in some kind of deposit that has a good liquidity, i. e., if the person needs money for the next half hour, can run up the agency and withdraw the demanded amount (Joan Robinson states that anyone who simply has deposited in a bank account was not investing, because who invests is one who takes that amount and use it on any production). Who still could not keep this bank fund needs to acquire the discipline to get this. And if the problem is very little gain, he must seek to earn more, be seeking a higher salary or creating a parallel means of earning a larger income, like those women who resell lingerie to their colleagues at work. Many financial managers recommend the *Fliche Technique*, as a training to reach an economically comfortable situation. What is this Fliche Technique? It is an acrostic, a mnemonic for a set of attitudes and requirements for achieving this condition:
- Friendship (cultivate friendships that help keep good jobs);
- Limit (set spending limit per period);
- Initiative (act promptly, not hoping for rain in the garden);
- Control (of what is needful and urgent or can delay);
- Habit (keep the habit of saving and making investments);
- Education (take courses that qualify you for greater gains).

# Chapter 7. The seven weaknesses

*Gluttony.* Should we worry about this problem of gluttony?

Because of the tradition of the Christian doctrine in the region, the seven weaknesses of the head, which in religion are the seven capital sins, are not a big problem for Latin Americans. Gluttony, by example, is cultivated in a smaller proportion than in the United States, and is restricted almost only to large urban centers where the ease of access to as varied as irresistible goodies controls the minds of the citizens who do not have much affinity with the cardinal virtues of Prudence, Fortress and Temperance (as has been said, the mnemonic of the four Aristotelian cardinal virtues is *Jusprufortem*: Justice, Prudence, Fortress and Temperance).

The seven capital sins, or sins of the head, are: gluttony, wrath, lust, greed, sloth, envy and pride (the mnemonic is *Gwlgsep*). Locating gluttony in the first place serves here two purposes, one being the composition of the mnemonic and other this of showing that, if the gluttony is neither a serious problem, other mental sins also nor are. But it never hurts repeat that this is due to the fact of it still to sound strong in the behavior of Latin Americans the Christian missionary work, from the first indigenous literacy courses at the region in the sixteenth century. There being relaxation in this indoctrination, nobody can guarantee that this capital will not be lost. So it's always wise to prevent.

The campaigns against obesity, which in the most of the cases is identified today as a medical problem, play the role of continuing condemning gluttony. But it would be better to keep this custom through cultural tradition, without needing to reach the contingency of using television or the Ministry of Health for campaigns.

*Wrath*. Is there risk of increasing wrath in society?

Many have the impression that the level of aggression has increased greatly in recent years, given the unquestionable increase in the volume of murders. Certainly, the violence increased, but not as much as it seems. It increased because the television virtually replaced the culture of friendliness by the culture of intolerance of certain American groups. Hence, the huge growth is this of the technology of death. Therefore, the sin of anger did not suffer increase in the society as big as people think, but the attacks with knives, who formerly led a small percentage of affected to death, were exchanged for assault helped by guns, which eventually cause death in the most of the cases.

This small increase in aggression must worry us, yes. The culture of children today is very different of that of children forty years ago. In the deformed "ethics" of small adolescents in this beginning millennium, is "wrong" to separate fights. When two unsuspecting slug, others should attend the battle - screaming exhortations as in cock fights - and never try to separate them. What the assistance wants to see is how much hurt the winner will impose to the overcome one.

Regardless of what it broadcasts, the television also makes young people impatient and, in some cases, intolerant persons. Like everything in it is resolved in the short term, and the information that the regular school only gives to the child after six or seven years of preparation are passed in it within minutes, the youth has developed a "pathos" of anxiety with which it has very difficult to deal with.

The exercise to overcome the sin of anger is the cultivation of patience, which is included in the virtue of Fortress. He who has strength of character is patient and tolerant, and so much hardly see himself taken by anger. Trying to understand the reasons to the other failures is the way to not irritate you yourself more than the reasonable.

If you go very cranky, caught out in anger state very often, then you can be too involved with a problem whose solution is not in sight. In this case, you should convince yourself that great solutions hardly depend on you alone, even if you are the head of government. And if others annoy you because they are delaying the arrival of this solution, always remember that they are not to blame for being barely able or uneducated.

*Lust.* Can lust become disease?

The sin of libertinism reaches small portion of Latin Americans, although these people are in general more sensuous than the population of most countries (there are those who confuse lust with vanity, because the first two letters of the word). Lust means overly libidinous behavior and, in the language of today, is best represented by "sexual abuse".

In the United States this is a problem that occurs with much greater frequency than in South America. There are, for example, the well-known case of actor Michael Douglas, Kirk Douglas' son, who was admitted to treatment for sexual incontinence.

Certainly, sex in alternate days is healthy, no longer being we able to say the same about daily and repetitive sex, what produces pimples on youth and boredom-of-routine in older. Young people lovers, in these times of anticipation and liberalization of sexual habits, need to be careful on the use of their libido.

The intelligence of the incipient human species destroyed the heat of the woman, turning her into sexual partner in any phase of the month or year. This was positive for giving a more motivation to the value of life, but we should never stop questioning us about the rightness of this drastic intervention in the nature. It is likely that this has served for decreasing the fights among men in the race of females in heat and, if so, then the decision of cohabitation with consequent dilution of receptivity period was something right and it was a wise move of our ancestors. Otherwise, if it was only by hedonism, we must continue with our doubts. Because a terrible result in the long run is the saturation of the Earth habitable capacity. Those who rejected Malthus without reading his texts were not aware of the problem scale raised by him. The countries that have reached of first this stage of the cohabitation in homes and so on conurbations constituted as cities are today in the bearable limit of the demographic crowding. Facilitating access to sex thus represented a violence against the nature and the accumulation of a debt that so heavy we can never be paid. The cost will be too high when the inevitable recovery, in the moment of the exhaustion of the planet's resources. Even before all this abundance of supply of sex, there are unsatisfied people, who always want more.

Those who indulge in lust do it by cultivating a romantic philosophy of overlapping the body on the intellect, or are victim of a disease, by which the actor Michael Douglas believed to have been affected. This second situation is rare in South America, although occasionally maniacs arise in the dark nights at the big cities, frightening the young girls who need to walk through the streets. Those with the disease are not subject to any tolerance by society, being seen even by prisoners, who never forgive them, as the worst scum of its kind.

But romantic lustful are just the result of a misdirected education. If this is your case, and hopefully you will not be considered luxurious, it is important that you take contact with higher philosophies, changing the sensuality and romanticism by doctrines like Stoicism and Platonic idealism, while also diving into the Pauline Christianity, provided by the necessary critical sense for a healthy understanding of ancient texts.

We have followed the trend of acquittal of the practices that until recently we called "sexual deviances". The exception has been the so-called "pedophilia". Before, an adult who got pregnant a minor teenage was forced to marry her, to form a family and take care of the offspring. At the current understanding (from the late twentieth century), this racy boy goes to the jail, leaving the minor and her offspring in the care of her maternal grandmother, when this grandmother agrees with the task. If the girl is pregnant by a minor age young, untouchable, it is expected that the grandmother takes care of the child and the boy remains free to get other children with other unsuspecting teenagers. The sex among minors is not more seen as a problem, since they are untouchable. Between an adult man and a minor teenage, this is intolerable in the understanding of the current codes. Among two or more adult persons, of age, anything goes and has become politically incorrect to mention the concept of "deviant". Now, there is a healthy sexual practice. It is very important that schools and parents instruct children about it, in a clear and decisive manner. Those who go beyond the limits of this sanity, for older they are, must do so because they can not overcome their drives, without involving healthy people in their experiences. If parents are unhappy because they see a child under age harassed by an older man of age, why will they have to see with good eyes this same harassment when their child is eighteen full years-old? Many will say that this age the child shall be master of his nose. Yes, but he should start a homosexual practice only if he is unable to overcome a likely drive that he is a carrier. Many boys are initiated in this practice without having any tendency for it, just to pay some tract against others who have already started on the subject. Families need to give clear guidance on these possibilities. No man will bugger before practicing sodomy, and he will not be while just imagine or want to be it. If he has no drive in this direction, he will be rid of the practice since he does not give up to the harassment of others, and for this a good guidance is essential. If he is prone, if he wants to have sex with people of his gender, even so we have not for granted that it will sound move from fantasy to the practice. If the therapist orders to carry out the alleged desire and the religious minister imposes to resist the temptation, so the boy has to take a crucial decision. If the therapist has knowledge of the facts to make that recommendation, then that's his point of view. He tried and approved that. It does not mean it will be good for the boy who is in doubt. If the therapist has neither experienced, nor from personal experience he has the authority to send the boy to the path of homosexuality. Many are horrified when they hear Catholic religious expose its position on the resistance to appeals of abusive sexual practices. But the rigidly dogmatic religious, those who made vows of chastity, not only learned to resist in front of sexual deviations appeals as well as to call of heterosexual, non-consanguineous, normal and universal sex. If anyone is qualified to preach resistance, this one is that religious person. Admittedly, he can be not a model for the sexual behavior of the lay individual. But the layman yet has in him the extreme example of control of the will (forget here the weak priests who shame the Catholic hierarchy). Nobody is driver because wanted to drive cars, no one is an architect because wished attend architecture and design houses, no one is a dentist because wished treat teeth, without practicing dentistry. So nobody is bugger because desired to practice sodomy, just as no one is pedophile because imagined him himself in sex scene with minors. Pedophile is someone who has done pedophilia, homosexual is who practiced homosexuality. Nobody can be convicted by imagining or wishing, although the desire is the capital sin (i. e., sin of the "caput", the head). The sense of the capital (cardinal) sin is: nourishing in the imagination a certain transgression leads to planning the action. So it is a sin, not a crime. How does one free from sin? Getting rid of desire, according to precepts of

Buddhism and of Mosaic religions. But if the crime is committed, there is no way to get rid of it, and one can only, at best, purge it, i. e., pay the punishment that perhaps anyone ministers to the case. All the discussion, all the tours on these issues have this sense: drives exist, appeals exist, harassment exist, and the willpower is the main asset of the individual in his moment of decision making. Cultivate and strengthen your willpower. Remember that puppet Pinocchio went through many difficulties before making his dream to become person because he easily fell into conversation of crooks. This book is about the four Aristotelian cardinal virtues, Justice, Prudence, Fortress and Temperance, but with emphasis especially in the virtue of the Fortress.

*Greed.* Is some degree of greed a good thing?

It is a cardinal sin that, by so rare among Latin Americans, confirms the strong "Imprinting" of the Christian preaching against all seven sins. Many are the citizens who try to get along in the trade, for example, and do not go forward due to lack of some stinginess. A trader who invested his meager savings in structure and goods has not the courage of denying spun to his acquaintances, who leads him to the ground in a few months. And many not even buy on credit, but earn free really.

It is no doubt that there is stingy Latin Americans. Everyone knows at least one who is able to give his life for a penny. Even so, the greedy are very few in number, and the modal behavior of our people is this of the generosity, blessed in every way, notwithstanding the prejudice of that unfortunate merchant.

Even the savings campaigns face not only the tendency to dissolution, but also the virtue of generosity.

If you tend to nourish the addiction of avarice, remember that saving is very important and it is right a matter of good education, but that the sound generosity, one that does not involve deformation of character of the poor, should never be abandoned. What we should combat really is the trend to waste and spending. A spendthrift individual is almost as unreliable as an alcohol dependent.

Laziness. How can I escape the temptation to become lazy?

Although many people believe that South Americans are given to laziness, this is a wrong impression. In the United States, South American immigrants are respected as working people, who does not show rejection of heavy work - what proves the effect of prejudice of compatriots in their own territory in Brazil and neighborhood when many refuse to "grab the hoe" in front of others.

Therefore, it is necessary that there is not confusion between laziness and refusal to manual work due to the alien prejudice. Eliminated the disease of the "chiro-ergophobia", we see that South Americans are so workers that, in a short time, the region will be in an enviable economic situation.

A huge risk that is running the South American diligence is the true situation of debacle in teaching. Under the bad education that has been provided to children by the South American education systems, children have developed a new trend to the breach of duties, what was to be expected (they are copied educational models of countries that have cultivated a bad education so that South Americans develop bad habits that did not have before).

The following recommendations serve for you and your near, if you perceive some bias toward the development of laziness.

You must accustom yourself to enter into mental commitments with yourself. An example is you to finish the work started. There is a very large number of people who start projects and leave along the way, without an ending. If you are here, do yourself a promise that you will complete your projects, and program yourself to make yourself the exigency when this promise will be not fulfilled. Another problem that toils in the daily life of many people is to delay projects, while having even the feeling that they will not have a term. A basic example is the writing of a book, more specifically of a thesis. Many complete graduate course and do not receive title, because they never get to finish their thesis. The remedy is similar to that given above: do promise that will complete the project. But here there is more. Seal the commitment from you to yourselves in order to work daily in the book making. In days with more enthusiasm and time multiple pages can be written. In poor days of inspiration, write a few lines. The important is to keep this commitment as a ritual to write at least one line every day. Within three months, a thesis will be written, surely.

If you have laziness to go out from your house to go to work, first think of the loss of giving up to this whim. But do not think only in specific prejudice of that moment. Think with best care of losses that will result from the processing of this trend in addiction. Also the lazy ones are almost as frowned upon as alcoholics.

*Envy*. Can I accept that others stimulate me to be envious?

Although generally South Americans are not envious, always as result of the Christian formation, there is some regions that cultivate this plague as their provincial defect. As the fail "looks like badly", its manifestation is often disguised and sometimes only after years living together with the person we found out he is envious.

The envious persons are feared because they are almost always individuals who do not focus efforts in their projects, dispersing their concerns with trying to follow the trail of others. In this practice of targeting others and envy them, often the target person feels dwarfed and this will give him the feeling that the influence of the envious individual pulls him down. It may even be that it pulls, by psychological mechanisms that we do not yet know.

The truth is that nobody wants an envious person as a companion, and even an envious one rejects it. Often the ape behavior is confused with envy and this is one more reason to do campaign against the Brazilian mania of copying.

In fact, the healing of envy goes through the same mechanism of the ape behavior cure. It is necessary to appreciate the originality, value the pursuit of the own path. The envious person has not this path and the ape wants not it. But it is necessary to pick it up and enjoy it.

If you think that sometimes you feel envy of others, remember that you are like the others just in format, as all of us belong to the human species. Your fingerprints are unique and your personality is unique too. If you feel unhappy for not being what others are or for not having what others have, understand that what the other has is nothing compared to what many millionaires have around. If you envy someone's car, think then that this unfortunate one may be envying the yacht of another richer. If you envy his way of being, think of the same as the relationship between him and another he finds superior. If you envy someone's fame, remember that freedom is much more important than this. Acquire the goods that are compatible with your personal characteristics, which are not the same as anyone else's. You must discipline yourself so that you feel yourself in a bad situation if you surprise yourself acquiring any product moved by envy. Some television advertisements seek to awaken the feeling of envy for selling certain products. Run away from them.

*Pride*. Can prejudiced people change their feeling?

Many people wonder if prejudice is not a capital sin. Yes, it is. All of the forms of prejudice are included in the great vice of superb. If is it very common among South Americans? Not among poor, the vast majority of people. But among the middle classes and the ruling class it shows his face here and there. Color prejudice, prejudice of class, prejudice against manual labor, all these defects are manifested as superb. If someone thinks himself above the others, naturally better than his neighbors, expressing it in gestures and decisions, this is an overwhelmed, who had the misfortune of receiving uneducated rules in the cradle, instead of education. And it is misfortune because, if there is something that takes away potential friends, it is the superb. Only those who have the same defect tolerate these figures. In the classrooms, a teenager or a youth with such a 'disorder' is rejected by colleagues like a kind of incommunicable extraterrestrial.

Living in very high luxury condominium, having custom of purchasing in shop of more overvalued products of the city and traveling never on public transport terrestrial vehicles, like bus and subway, they are a safe step for the development of the superb. For the condominium that was thought safe is in the hands of robbers as much as any cheap condominium, the costly products of sophisticated store are the same as those common in stores with prices that do not reach ten percent of these there and the urban bus, although very crowded at certain times, leads to all of the important points of the city. Anyone traveling in them gives evidence that does not feel rejection by the proximity of the citizens of popular classes.

If you paid expensive schools for your children, you know very well that you are not looking for good teaching, but for exclusion, even if you have other reasons. You want to prepare them into place where the poor and the dark skin are excluded. If you think that in this expensive schools there is more security, you're wrong, because it has 25% drug users, compared to 5% in state schools, like serious research already conducted. The argument that public or community schools have low education quality do not free you, for this poor quality is caused exactly by the abandonment by those who used this reasoning before. The more the middle class get away from the public school, seeking unconscious or surreptitiously cultivate pride, more the quality of education for both varieties will be impaired because there is only good education in situation of democratic life, where meritocracy is essential element. And the argument that it is the Catholic Church that requires continuing basic education in the hands of "paid schools" is not justified, because, in France, Catholic faith schools do not charge fees, and their teachers are paid by the government, without Vatican restrictions on the present system.

It is the involvement of parents, first of all, that raises the quality of education in community school. If parents think the school's role is to keep locked their children and to ensure their approval at any cost in all of the subject matters, cheering former teachers and demagogic politicians who feed this perversion, then there is no way to improve teaching, even in private and expensive education, in countries where this is allowed. If, however, they accept the democratic access and meritocracy - not the formation of homogeneous classes - and have aware that the school role for their children is to prepare them for the freedom of choice, with possession of the content domain and the skills that young people acquire in the best schools of the world, so they are able to demand and obtain a good school in their neighborhood.

Prejudices are as non-removable obstacles. These should not be destroyed, but circumvented. A person who cultivates color prejudice will not change his feeling even under very strong religious indoctrination. Nothing prevents, however, that a racist person becomes polished, and the output is exactly this.

The mere discussion of racism may represent nothing more than racist practice and it is only acceptable when dealing with the attempt to search mechanisms to overcome the problem, i. e., of equality assurance, in practice.

The crime of racism is not about feeling, but demonstration. Between two individuals, a slightly racist and other terribly racist, the first will be arrested if he manifests his impressions, while the second one, if he is polite and keeps to him himself his harmful feelings, acting with equanimity, he will be free of any punishment. If this polished individual refrains from express his racism in front of his children, he shall transmit to them not only his politeness, but also the absence of the sickening feeling of racism.

# Chapter 8. The four paths

So that you may be a person endowed with willpower, there are several ways. The easiest paths are more effective, but less efficient. Costly paths are really efficient, though less effective. (Effective is what leads to achieve the result without consideration of cost; efficient is what consistently leads to goal through good use of resources.)

In the analysis of success-failure factors, paths suffer interference from two fronts: external factors and internal factors. Among the external factors we include that of the material type, when the scarcity or abundance of supply of the product you want to set free disrupts your strategies, and that of the affective type, when your chances of making use of a path receive positive or negative influences of people who are around you. In general the spouse and close relatives, as well as friends, are essential elements in the construction of the cardinal virtue of fortitude in the individual. If a person stopped smoking the day before, for example, and receives compliments and wishes for success from relatives and friends, his chances of keeping the purpose significantly increase compared to someone who has not received any word and any gesture of support from people nearby.

Anticipating Maslow, by emphasizing always the need for external recognition as a value highest in shaping the behavior of the child, a professor of Wisconsin wrote: "The mere consciousness of his own ability (to his mind, his own worth) does not furnish him with sufficient pleasure; it must be reinforced by actual recognition from others." (The Psychology of Conduct - Hermann Henry Schroeder, State Normal School, Whitewater, Wis., Chicago Row, Peterson & Company, 1911.)

It is very common the case of the boy who stopped drinking a few days ago and, unluckily, met with old mates of drunkenness, properly equipped with the liquid he tried to flee. The two kinds of external factors were present: material supply and the affective invitation. In a typical case, a lady was arrested some time ago because it was discovered that she had kept tied her minor son, who was addicted to drugs. With the mother prison, the son rescued the freedom of which his mother went depriving him and in a few weeks he died. As the legal and political system had not healthy alternative to the attitude of that mother, who acted to prevent the son kept in touch with external factors that came destroying him, its action to punish that mother simply had the role of expediting the anticipated tragedy. It was seen there the foolish use of law against the use of the principle of the lesser evil.

It is known that motivation is intrinsic to the individual, and therefore nobody motivates anyone. But people encourage them themselves to each other in order to obtain successful in their enterprises. With this encouragement coming from emotionally close people, always gets easier to achieve a goal. The burden is lighter, however, when the exhortation comes in sense of weakness ("Drink at least one cup there to keep us company") and the entire effort can undo in the air like a very full plastic balloon that suddenly finds the tip of a pin.

As for the internal forum of decisions, dependent on internal factors, the easy-effective and specific way is that of the religious conversion. If you allow indoctrinating by the practice of a coded religion, your holy book will give you guidelines to overcome the temptations that push for addictions. The output is effective because the person's mind will be well protected by the doctrine. But is not efficient because the sound exercise of the doubt can be fatal to the strategy. And the person should not forget that if he creates prayers, spiritual messages or even secular poetry, he must first, before saying them, write them down with eyes closed (if it is in the computer, he can look at the screen, but not the keyboard), for getting rid of the "universal eye", which is the possible perversion of interpretation that the unconscious of mankind produces. It's unknown just the thing which has never been seen by any human eye. Religion is neither a joke, nor a walk.

The most expensive-efficient and general way is philosophy, always grounded in scientific results. But between these two extremes we have the middle ground of politics, whether by trade union, whether by party, and the entrepreneurship.

In politics there is high degree of effectiveness, especially for people less independent, because almost always a guru-educator, or a group of them, serves as guide to the neophyte and give him a supposedly healthy set of behavioral norms.

In the entrepreneurship the grade of how effectiveness gives way to efficiency, because the citizen has to develop methods to achieve goals, while knowing that the chance of success is closely tied to the development of his own way.

In trade, for example, he cannot progress without abandoning the wasteful practice. And although there are still cases of large traders with drugged sons, one cannot grow in trade spending on drug use. Therefore, the decision to become an entrepreneur leads to the intellectual discipline that results in the cultivation of a consistent willpower.

The field of the instructional philosophy, which sees with deep critical base the inferior stages of political romanticism, cynicism and hedonism, it is, ultimately, the efficient and superior path that one must walk to the conquest of the willpower possession.

It should be taken into account that "philosophy" today means "scientific methodology". One can walk this path without need of religious practice (if one does not have it), without trade union or party meetings and without becoming business agent. It is therefore the way to freedom.

So, the (a) religious, (b) political, (c) entrepreneurial and (d) philosophical paths represent a progressive scale, which does not mean that one must go through it from one end to another, necessarily. Each person must seek out what suits him best. However, when reaching not the instructive and philosophical way, one should always keep in mind that any fanaticism is the opposite of willpower.

# Appendix
# Distillates: five centuries of cirrhosis
(A plea to the leaders of the clergy)

Inebriety existed for millennia. What there is new in this history is the alcoholism, which only grew after the invention of the distilled alcoholic drink, in 1498, in England.

*Food.* Many reports can be read on drunken people in the previous centuries, but the use that was done of the fermented alcoholic drinks was that one of alimentary complement - beer, wine and sake were drinks swallowed with meals - or that one of exciting element in parties. The history of the individual dependent on alcohol, who sustains the owner of the tavern while has income for this, it began on that year 1498, with the distillates.

*Lies.* He who, drunk, provokes accident of traffic and says he just drank a beer can, he lies; yes, the can was consumed, but accompanying doses of distillates, because a beer alters, when a lot, reflexes of a beginner, of somebody who never has ingested alcoholic drink, not of somebody who has already drunk before. He who says that the effect of the beer and of the wine is the same of the distillates, lies too. He who is fallen in the sidewalk for inebriety and says that he only has ingested beer, he lies in the same way. Of course the same molecule of alcohol is found in distilled and in fermented drinks and, for this reason, former-alcoholic have to avoid as much one as other. But the ones who lose the job for alcoholism and destroy the own family, they never did it by ingesting just fermented drunk; distillate is the problem.

*Darkness.* If some thing in the modernity was invented under inspiration of the malign spirit, this was the distillate. As destructive potential, it has in the body the effect of the caustic soda, although its action is very slow. It's already the moment of stopping to deal with it as drink, for beginning to see it as "industrialized caustic water".

*Freedom.* Muslims and Pentecostals get to maintain their followers far away from the alcoholism equaling and condemning fermented and distilled. That kills, through religion, a tradition of millennia, which is the one of having meals accompanied of fermented drinks, and it impedes the individual's freedom of tasting drinks that are not malicious.

*Prohibition.* The Dry Law, in the United States, suffered of that harmful faith that distilled and fermented cause the same damage. Besides, it didn't take into account that dependent on alcohol would seek offenders to satisfy their needs. The prohibition has been, therefore, sabotaged, and, ever since, trying to eliminate the distillates of the western ethylic habit became taboo.

*Drivers.* Suddenly in the turning of the millennium all of the citizens became almost drivers of their own vehicles. Alcoholic drink in the direction of automobiles has begun to be one of the great causes of deaths by accidents. The one that the governments have been doing is to fine who uses alcoholic drink, fermented or distilled, and goes driving. In this it is going implicit the idea that there is no problem in drinking, since one doesn't go soon to drive. The governments are, so, spoiling the population. Drinking distilled is, yes, a purposeless action. If the individual argues that he has right on the own liver, he should be alerted that distillates are a first problem to his family and to his job place, if it is true that he still has room in the family and in the work.

*Catholic.* Catholics without catechetical formation can be convinced easily to embrace religions that condemn the ingestion of the fermented drinks. But Catholics of solid base won't be affected with such a preaching. However, they don't see the brutal difference between a cognac dose and a glass of wine. They has not been informed that the distilled drink is what will turn them dependent and will destroy their liver, pulling off their job and their family, thing that the wine and the beer, without distillates, will never do. It is time of us to do clear those points. It will be good that the Catholic Church helps the governments condemning the distillates, without attacking the fermented drinks. While both types of drinks will be seen as equally harmful, nothing will get better. The parish priests should proclaim their followers the evils of that terrible invention that is the distilled alcohol used not as a fuel, but as drink. Parents should indoctrinate their children early against the confusion of seeing in a destructive chemical product, which is the distilled alcohol, whether of cane, grape, banana, potato, malt or corn, a drink that can bring happiness or comfort, when he only brings unhappiness for the relatives and friends, and slow death for whom ingests it.

# Afterword - "The dew comes falling"

This is a book about behavior, practical application for the Psychology of Conduct, not a self-help book. Nobody motivates anyone. What one can do is to stay informed and thereby trying to awaken the dormant potential within the person.

The study in Business Administration and the experience in teaching with basic subject matters in high school gave to this author broad training in observing how young people behave, from what he extracted valuable and numerous lessons, which now shares with the reader.

Certainly some points in the book may seem strange, even contrary to good sense. But when this is the case, the reader is invited to replace "common sense" with "common traditional sense". What seems incongruous is often only incompatible with standards that we are accustomed to experience, without question.

Almost the entire contingent of individuals making the street their home, sleeping on sidewalks or on lawns, is composed of alcoholics. There are also those who were brought to this condition for use of narcotics and those sleeping outside on a temporary basis due to extreme poverty, waiting for some jobs. The latter ones form a minority contingent.

Whatever the reason that has led the individual to sleep on the street, it is known by the more experienced ones in this vicissitude that they ought not sleep at night, if the location of the rest is the center of any big city. Those who have knowingly sleep during the day, because in nighttime neo-Nazis swarm always ready to burn or kill the homeless individuals who make the risk of sleeping at this time, when the street gets emptied of the persons flow. The sacrificed ones use to be those very poor migrants, newcomers and uninformed. If in residential areas away from the city center the homeless receive some protection from neighbors, and even from the night watchman, it is not this what happens in the central region, no man's land. There, neo-Nazis call the shots. The drunken and the dependent on other drugs often sleep at night by having not more self-control and, even when are knowledgeable of the dangers to their condition, are exposed to the slaughter.

Aware rulers seek to remove from the center of large cities - leading to hostels, hospitals or other less bloody areas - these potential victims of those unbalanced ones. But they know they will have to face the barriers of law and even the shouting of certain romantic persons, those who take the protection to the disadvantaged with attempts of cleaning the territory, calling this policy "hygienist", in ironic sense. They fight with all the courage to keep homeless individuals sleeping in areas of danger, but when these persons are killed they disappear lime ether. They do not want to be accused of killer's allies.

Dealing specifically on alcohol, banning distillates to adolescents and releasing them without restriction to those of age is the tradition, but it is not the best way to discourage the attraction that young people feel for this product. The most efficient way to minimize attractiveness is to create obstacles for the elderly, making it clear that to the young man it is allowed because is not expected much responsibility from him, but rather that he has a chance and time to mature. Even so, the person over 21 years old, who has not permission to pay for doses at the bar, can buy sealed bottles in the supermarket and take home. And to inhibit also this form of purchase, the tax burden on distillates should be at least the double of that imposed on fermented alcoholic beverages. The supervision and punishment on illegal vendors, who will take advantage of restrictions, should be hardened.

Why a total ban does not work? What led to the failure of the Dry Law in the United States is very easy to understand. When it came to ban there were many people dependent. They came to pay any price for the product, which could no longer get legally. The offenders were made rich, and the business, which was illegal, out of reach the arm of law, was ruled by bandits. Al Capone could only be arrested for inconsistency in the income tax statement. Thus, the most appropriate in this case is to difficult the acquisition, not to prohibit. And this difficulty, provoked, cannot have any breakdown that makes glamorous to search for the item. If a special taxation arising overpricing brings this distortion, it may be useful to give it up and release the sale for over 21, in pharmacies, only, and uniquely to individuals who are under medical treatment for addiction. The transformation of the problem that today is social and moral in essentially medical problem is a parting shot in the era of distillates.

A person who wants to get rid of alcohol dependence should not continue to grow friendships around him in the days of misfortune, unless those friendships follow that decision, which is not uncommon. Former alcoholics who are released in communion strengthen their ties of friendship and give each other support in degree that outsiders to the problem never would do. On through a severe storm, a castaway can save some companions, but it has limits. If he tries to save a lot more people than what his forces can support, all of them will go to background. And from that fellow who instead of helping is, on the contrary, doing much strength to pull down those who try to save him, the best thing to do is to escape. This is an act of legitimate defense of life itself. The opening sentence of this book, ensuring that "the pillar of willpower is the support of friends", is meaningless when it comes to seek support in friends who do not have anything to offer in terms of determination. Friends who do not have the strength to pull himself together, to improve their own condition, they can either encourage others. What a friend of these can offer is wise advice: "Look at my sorry state and search another type of friendship."

A castaway (still a castaway) that is alone on an island and rest assured that he will not see any more similar in his future days will have no incentive to positive actions beyond those that mean the struggle for survival. He will not have motive to shave every day or to wear clean and fragrant linen regularly. It is the prospect of meeting friends or a possible future girlfriend that will take you to get ready, so that you have contributions to make. This meeting is the key to optimism. An incorrigible optimist is a fool, because certainly he does not take into account that everything we do is a pastime in the trajectory to the dissolution of our flesh, once there ahead we will dissolve us ourselves, leaving only our skeleton, which in future centuries will also be dissolved, if not cremated before. But the incorrigible pessimistic is in much more uncomfortable situation, because he does not see with optimism the possibility of bequeathing to his similar ones a positive contribution. Mother Hildegard, at the twelfth century, if the reporting of biographers is reliable, rose from the deathbed, when already were being watched, and resumed her activities, alleging that she still had contributions to make. Writer and political Darcy Ribeiro, already old and admitted to the hospital, jumped the window and returned home because he still had a project that could not leave, which was to write the book "The Brazilian people". The optimism about the future and about building a more advanced society, as part of our evolution, serves therefore as a counterpoint to the natural pessimism that we cultivate across the finiteness of our individual existence.

He who has doubts about the evolution of social and political organization of nations must pay attention to the fact that the twentieth century abolished the three major behavioral plagues that tormented us: slavery, official racial discrimination and conventional war (it lacks now the elimination of the involuntary unemployment.)

A bird made a nest on a unsafe branch. The puppy was almost ready to fly away. It came a very strong wind and the branch where the nest was has been hit by another branch, knocking the puppy, which fell on a rock and died instantly. There are not many millennia mankind has been subjected to such whims of fortune and to the cruel hand of the natural selection. Many think we should go back to that time.

He who does not conform to human progress insists on giving old names to new phenomena. Slavery, for example, was an economic system in which a man had, officially, the property of people. If an individual sequesters other and forces him to work, the name of this is servile work, not "slave labor", as some persons want. Official racial discrimination was extinct in the United States and in South Africa, ending its era, although some governments still insist on installing racial discrimination with a supposed opposite sign, like in India and up even in some federal units of the United States, imagining to be doing something good to the harmed ones. As for war, the twenty-first century ushered in September 2001, with the attack on the twin towers in New York, the new type of "warlike" conflict in the world: confrontation caused by unsuspecting flocks led by religious fanatics. Calling it "war", as George Walker Bush did, is not to accept the signs of change, acutely envisioned by Prof. Francis Fukuyama. The conventional war, regular army against regular army, exhausted at the end of the twentieth century. With this objective the United Nations was created, after the failure of the ephemeral League of Nations.

# Synthesis

* The four paths to the individual self-control: religion, politics, entrepreneurship, philosophy (from the easier-specific and effective to the harder-general and efficient).

* The four Aristotelian virtues: Justice, Prudence, Fortitude and Temperance (*Jusprufortem*).

* The seven weaknesses of the head (capital sins): gluttony, wrath, lust, greed, sloth, envy, pride (prejudice). Mnemonic: *Gwlgsep*.

* The five mental bandages that we have to get rid of:
- *Conductive:* super-mother – guru-pedagogue - idolatry
- *Illusionist:* passion - fanaticism
- *Acquisitive:* theft - robbery - alms - embezzlement
- *Compulsive:* drugs - addictions - game - interest - Advertising
- *Psychosomatic:* obesity - negligence - shyness - self-destruction

cacildomarques@gmail.com

@cacildo

www.ingramcontent.com/pod-product-compliance
Lightning Source LLC
Chambersburg PA
CBHW071220280526
45787CB00002B/746